# passion

# passion

## THE BRIGHT LIGHT OF GLORY

Louie Giglio

W Publishing Group
An Imprint of Thomas Nelson

Published in Nashville, Tennessee, by W Publishing, an imprint of Thomas Nelson.

Thomas Nelson titles may be purchased in bulk for educational, business, fund-raising, or sales promotional use. For information, please e-mail SpecialMarkets@ThomasNelson.com.



**Library of Congress Control Number: 2013921100**

ISBN 978-0-5291-1011-4

*Printed in the United States of America*

14 15 16 17 18 RRD 7 6 5 4 3

*Yes, Lord, walking in the way of Your truth,*
*we wait eagerly for You, for Your name and*
*Your renown are the desire of our souls.*
*—Isaiah 26:8*

# Contents

# Introduction

It's a quiet fall afternoon outside Memphis, and a gentle breeze is blowing as the sun pours down on a grassy expanse called Shelby Farms. Now part of a beautiful public park, this land is a special place for all connected to the Passion story and is the perfect place to begin our journey in this book.

In days gone by this rolling field was actually farmed by prisoners as part of a nearby correctional facility. But on a misty Saturday in May 2000, this very dirt became holy ground—possibly the most sacred earth on which I have ever walked. If you were there, one of the forty thousand college-aged young people who knelt here on that day, I have a feeling you are nodding in agreement. It was a day that marked our hearts forever, and a day that shaped the future of Passion.

Barely four years old at the time, the Passion Movement was sprouting fast and on this day we had invited the college-aged young people of our nation to join together for a solemn assembly. Our aim was not to simply host a festival, concert, or event. In fact, the publicity did not even include the names of speakers or bands. That felt like a crazy idea at the time, but we didn't care. The invitation was to come and meet with God . . . to come and pray for an awakening in our generation. We found our rallying cry in the words of the prophet Joel:

Blow the trumpet in Zion,
 declare a holy fast,
 call a sacred assembly.
Gather the people. (Joel 2:15–16)

Why did we want to call for a gathering like this? Because our hearts were breaking for the university students of America—seventeen million of them at the time—most of whom, according to their own admission, did not know the Savior or even see a great need for one.

Though Passion was growing exponentially, jumping from 2,000 attendees at our first conference in 1997 to 5,000 the following year and 11,500 the year after that, the math still was not in our favor. Campuses were filled with a wealth of personal freedom, intellectual opportunity and social dynamics, but hearts were empty, foolishness rampant, and a void of true purpose and meaning only echoed the growing need for the name of Jesus to be known. We wanted them all to have the chance to know about Him, to hear the name of Jesus. We longed for them to know of His love for them and His power to awaken what lay dormant in hearts dulled by sin, and His ability to restore and even redeem what had been broken in their lives. We ached for it. But even if we kept the pace, doubling and expanding and filling more venues, we still didn't have time to reach seventeen million of them before they walked the graduation stage and the moment was lost.

So what should we do next? That's the question we asked as we sought God for the next step we should take. We had known from the beginning that our calling was to be a fuse—an igniter that would hopefully contribute to revival coming to the campuses of our land. We longed to see Jesus' name fill the mouths of His people, and to see Jesus get the praise He deserves.

In fact, we were so intoxicated by His name—and our amazing privilege of making it great with our lives—that we didn't even call the solemn assembly at Shelby Farms *Passion*. Rather, it was most commonly known as *OneDay2000*, a day set aside for the Lord. We intended to bow our faces to the earth (rain or shine) and ask God to have mercy on us, and our generation.

To get the word out we blanketed the nation for the nine months leading up to May. Our road reps (three hearty guys in an RV with a giant orange OneDay logo plastered on its side) racked up thousands of miles, rolling onto campuses at times with an invitation from a church or campus group and at others with nothing but the leading of the Spirit. Meanwhile, the OneDay campus tour was doing the same, hosting one-night rallies on 120 campuses from coast to coast. The call? Get to Memphis and represent your dorm, your campus, your church, your city, your generation. It felt like a Jesus version of Woodstock as we called people to do whatever it would take to kneel with their generation on this field.

To anchor the journey we hosted eight regional events in cities like Minneapolis/St. Paul, Seattle, San Jose, and one in the Agricultural Arena at Shelby Farms. That night is one that's hard to forget, and was a tad too foretelling. All day it dumped rain in epic proportion. Throughout the event it stormed like mad and suddenly with one massive clap of thunder the power went out. In an instant east Memphis went dark, including the arena.

The music stopped and the room went silent. Yet, after a moment of us all trying to figure out what was going on the crowd decided to keep on singing. If you've ever been in a moment like that you know at times the worship (singing) can feel even more determined without any production elements to assist. That's what it felt like in the arena on this night. Storm or no storm, we were going to worship Jesus together.

Eventually, the power surged on just as we were singing about God's mercy and grace. At first, the only thing working was a group of lights illuminating a cross at center stage. As we sang in a darkened arena the only light to be seen reflected brightly on the very symbol of our salvation. Needless to say, a roar went through the arena. We were on our way to OneDay2000, doing our best to prepare the way for the Son of God. We were hoping the brightness of His glory would break into the darkness of our campuses, awakening us to what life is really all about.

—Louie Giglio

# The Story of Passion

LOUIE GIGLIO

## Early Seeds Planted

"You know God is bringing you to Baylor for a reason," she said calmly. Have you ever been in one of those conversations where something was said and suddenly you knew God was in the equation? That's what happened by a lazy Texas river at an end-of-summer retreat with a group of college students I was working with in Houston. After lunch I ended up across the table from an amazing rising sophomore at Baylor, a Jesus-loving Tri Delta (that's a sorority) named Kay Dossey. Kay had recently had her own personal awakening to a real and personal relationship with Jesus. She was a leader on campus and had huge faith in God and a vision of what He could do in the lives of those around her.

For me, I had finished seminary in Fort Worth that spring and was entering another grad program at Baylor in a few days' time. (It might also be added that I was dating a Texan by the name of Shelley Graves who also attended Baylor and was at this same retreat.) During the past few summers, I had been leading as an intern to college students at two different churches in Houston. Kay had been a part of what had been happening in the summers as a growing band of collegians would return home each year for a few short months. We were seeking God with everything we had, packing out any available living room to dig into Scripture and worship together. Kay wanted to see what we were experiencing in Houston happen back at Baylor. And somehow she was convinced I was a part of God's plan.

Without telling the whole story, Kay's statement to me across the table that day in 1985 sparked a movement among the students of Baylor. On any given Monday night, it wasn't unusual to see 1,000 to 1,500 students who were on a new journey of worship and walking in the truth of God's Word. What I thought would be a two-year grad stint turned into a ten-year season of sharing life daily with college students, years that Shelley and I consider some of the most special of our lives.

Maybe something similar has happened to you. You weren't sure what path you were going to be on, but while looking at several options, God landed you in a place you didn't even see coming. That's what happened to Shelley and me. While we were wondering what was next in life after that graduate program, God was planting us at a critical intersection in the lives of college students—a place we have come to call the "university moment."

What became so clear to us in those years as we were pouring into and leading the students of Baylor, and as I was speaking to other campus groups across the nation, was that the university window of time is one of the most, if not *the most,* critical season in life. For most college students, the first semester at school is the first time they've been away from home—distant from the influences and people that have shaped their lives, with less accountability than ever and a wide array of choices regarding morality, beliefs, and values. Statistics show that for a vast number of Christians this terrain is difficult to navigate, something I can attest to from years of firsthand experience.

Why is it so difficult for young Christians to make the jump from the youth group back home to the campus environment? Why is it that a faith that seemed so sure in our adolescent years can quickly erode and sometimes even vanish? For one, in the campus climate students are faced with temptations that at times well-meaning people have attempted to shield them from in the past. They are assaulted by intellectual challenges to their worldview and beliefs that they may not be thoroughly prepared for. In the end, the question that starts to crack the foundation is this: is what I am carrying my faith or my parents' faith? Another way of asking it might be, is this what I believe or just what everybody at the church back home believed? Is Jesus real to me, or did I just have a mild dose of religion because that's what everyone else was doing?

Having been there year in and year out, we saw a lot of kids that were all fired up in the youth group implode within six weeks of moving into the dorm. Fortunately, we also watched as a lot of students who had walked away from what they had thought was faith truly find Jesus in a meaningful personal way before they graduated. But the reality is that most do not. And this is critical because the relationships and experiences forged while on campus shape so much of the trajectory of our lives. Like never before, a desire was stirring in us to stand at the crossroads of the "university moment" and do whatever we could to introduce people to the real and living Jesus.

## From a Campus to the Nation

You should never count God out. What He has planned and dreamed for your life far exceeds the circumstances of your day. He is always at work, painting on a canvas bigger than we can see or imagine. Not only is this true today; it's been true of our entire story to this point.

While we thought we were going to be leading students at Baylor for a very short season, God had another plan. At the end of each school year, we would sit with our Board and ask God if He was going to renew our assignment for another year. Nine times He said *yes.* We never set out to be at Baylor for a decade; we just found ourselves being available to Him *again*—nine times in a row.

But all that changed in 1994. That fall we sensed God saying it was time to go to Atlanta and help my mom take care of my dad who had been disabled by a brain disease seven years before. We were happy to go. Not happy about leaving what we loved, but relieved because we so desperately wanted to help my family in an intensely difficult time.

We did what we thought best. We put in place a transition for our staff and stayed through the end of the spring semester. But then something happened we could not have seen coming. On April 28, my father died suddenly of heart failure, unrelated to all the battles he had faced as part of the brain disease. On the day that our ministry at Baylor hosted our ten-year going-away celebration, Shelley and I were in Atlanta burying my dad.

Talk about being confused. Our hearts were shattered by the loss of my dad—crushed in a way I could never have fathomed before. Though we could have and should have lost him several times along the way, I was in no way prepared for the excruciating pain. And more, we thought somehow we had completely missed God's timing and plan by staying in Texas when we should have come straight away to be with my family in the fall.

Shelley and I were unsure, unemployed, uprooted, and now plopped down in a new city without a clear mission or purpose. But God had a plan all along. Within a few months a vision flashed in my heart that took our breath away. It wasn't a picture of one campus seeking God—it was the vision of a sea of young people on their faces before God, crying out for revival in the land.

I told Shelley what happened, but the experience was so unusual that I waited a few weeks to share it with anyone else. After a while we convened with our Board and a few others who had offered counsel in our lives. Everyone was nodding along, somehow all sensing the same urging and timing of God. Was all the heartache for this? Were we uprooted from what we had poured so much into at Baylor so God could more easily pluck us for a new assignment?

Have you ever felt like that, or are you are in a place like that right now? While I don't know your circumstances, I do know that God always has something in mind. I firmly believe that the following chapters from these incredible communicators are going to speak directly to your heart in unforeseen ways. Most often, the trials we are walking through today are preparing us for a greater role in God's unfolding story.

## Why Passion?

Over the course of the next few months, we talked with a few friends and campus leaders and eventually set out on a course to pursue the picture from the vision—because at this point, the image didn't come with a detailed how-to plan. Along with Cheryl Bell and Jeff Lewis, we rallied around a name that we felt best embodied this emerging gathering. We called it *Passion.*

All these years later, the name fits so well. But on day one it was a risk. Passion wasn't anywhere on the landscape of branding or cultural currency in 1995, except in an area of web domains we didn't want anyone to explore. But our team quickly rallied around a definition of Passion that spoke to the heart of what we wanted to be about:

> **Passion**—*the degree of difficulty we are willing to endure to accomplish the goal.*

That's it! For us, passion does not simply denote enthusiasm, zeal, or emotion. Passion conveys the gritty determination to finish the task at hand. That's why the final days of Jesus' life on earth are known as *Passion Week.* Passion is about doing whatever it takes to get what's most important to you. And what we wanted most was for Jesus' name to be echoed throughout the land.

Our name was set, yet the framework of our vision was still coming together. How would we get there? How would our message be refined? And then it happened. God literally dropped His Word in our laps. After speaking to a group of college students at a statewide event in Arkansas, I returned to my seat as the responsive worship was happening. I had given everything I had in that talk, calling us to live for the glory of God. I sat down next to the director of the event, and as I did, he plopped his Bible in my lap, a rather large, worn edition, opened to a passage in Isaiah.

I was slightly annoyed because I really wanted to fully lean into the song we were singing, but he insisted I see what he was showing me, firmly landing his finger on a highlighted verse. Slowly my eyes crossed the words . . .

"Yes, Lord, walking in the way of your laws, we wait for you; your name and renown are the desire of our hearts."

His finger was resting on Isaiah 26:8, but it might as well have been the finger of God. In those words we found our banner. We now knew what God was calling us to be about. He was inviting us to inspire a generation to live for His renown.

Those words leapt off the page—His renown. At the time I wasn't really sure what renown was all about, but a quick glance at the dictionary explains: *renown is fame or memory that will never fade away.*

We later morphed two translations into the phrase: *Yes, Lord, walking in the way of your truth we eagerly wait for you, for your name and renown are the desire of our souls.* To this day, this confession is our core, an unchanging beacon we seek to live out and proclaim to the world.

## Back to Memphis

So on the day students started arriving at Shelby Farms for OneDay2000, we could sense that God was going to meet us on that field in a powerful way. The main area was cordoned off from everyone, empty except for a tower built in the middle from which students read the Word of God nonstop for over twenty-four hours before the main gathering began. Then, on Saturday, we asked students to come prayerfully, reverently, soberly onto the field. And they did.

The clouds hung low that morning as 40,000 students and leaders settled on the hillside. Waiting. Believing. Expecting.

The day was unusual in so many ways. For one, according to one of the local TV weather reporters, an approaching thundercloud arriving on the edge of Shelby Farms suddenly split in two, traveling on each side of the field without dumping its fury on us all. On another occasion, a huge wooden cross was brought out before the people as Scriptures of mercy and grace were read over the people. At one point a young girl started running—sprinting—toward the stage and for the cross. I'd seen people "come forward" in all my years of church life, but I had never seen anyone sprint forward to reach out for the symbol of the cleansing flow of Jesus. After a while, students took hold of the cross and began to pass it overhead across the field, not as a way of worshipping an icon, but as a way of exalting what Christ had done for us.

But possibly the most stunning moment of all came after a pre-gathering prayer involving many of the speakers and leaders. Kneeling and standing in a tent beside the massive stage, after the final amen, no one wanted to move, and no one was eager to walk on the stage. It truly did feel holy, and though a huge crowd was waiting, we were all reluctant to walk on the stage. I recall someone saying, "Why don't you go up and lead first." And the reply, "No, you go." I knew when humans were acting like that that we really were on holy ground.

Something happened that day that changed us all. I believe that this movement, and even this book, got much of its start on that day, on those grounds, in the brightest light of His glory that we'd ever seen.

Almost twenty years later, many of the venues and faces have changed since our first gathering in Austin and the assembly at Shelby Farms. Our team has had the privilege of hosting worship events in locations ranging from an athletic field in Kampala to the finest performing arts center in Tokyo, from a velodrome in Cape Town to a football stadium in Atlanta. We've gathered students in fields, arenas, churches, conferences centers, and campus auditoriums on six continents. But while the places we have gathered have varied over the years, the message has remained the same. In fact, there has been a lot of consistency to this story, especially from the standpoint of those who have led with us on the Passion Team and those who have been on this journey with us from the beginning. When we arrived at that field in Memphis (and were praying in that tent that morning), Chris Tomlin, Charlie Hall, Nathan and Christy Nockels, and Matt Redman were already on board, leading alongside Sam Perry, Shelley Nirider, and a host of others, and helping forge the path with their songs of worship. John Piper spoke that day, giving an unforgettable message that has become a pillar of his ministry, called "Don't Waste Your Life." At the time, John was one of the few people I knew who was casting a vision for what it meant to desire God more than life itself and to glorify Him by our satisfaction in Him above all things.

Beth Moore spoke as well at OneDay2000 and has been a part of nearly every national gathering since she arrived with us in Austin in 1997. She has not just opened the Word of God in powerful ways, but she has been an avid supporter of our gatherings and mission.

Francis Chan, Christine Caine, and Judah Smith have also freely lent their voices to our movement in recent years, for which I am deeply grateful. They are dear friends and amazing instruments in the hands of God.

In the pages that follow, you will read some of the most impactful messages ever delivered to Passion-goers over the years. These chapters have never before been published in this format, and we believe you are going to be encouraged and challenged by these friends and leaders who were so excited to contribute both to Passion and this book.

Regardless of whether you had heard of Passion before opening this book, and regardless of your age and background, I believe that God has something to say to all of us about the beauty that comes from desiring his renown.

2

# Boasting Only in the Cross

JOHN PIPER

The opposite of wasting your life is living life by a single God-exalting, soul-satisfying passion. The well-lived life must be God-exalting and soul-satisfying because that is why God created us (Isaiah 43:7; Psalm 90:14). And "passion" is the right word (or, if you prefer, zeal, fervor, ardor, blood-earnestness) because God commands us to love him with *all* our heart (Matthew 22:37), and Jesus reminds us that he spits lukewarm people out of his mouth (Revelation 3:16). The opposite of wasting your life is to live by a single, soul-satisfying passion for the supremacy of God in all things.

How serious is this word "single"? Can life really have that much "singleness" of purpose? Can work and leisure and relationships and eating and lovemaking and ministry all really flow from a single passion? Is there something deep enough and big enough and strong enough to hold all that together? Can sex and cars and work and war and changing diapers and doing taxes really have a God-exalting, soul-satisfying unity?

This question drives us to the death of Jesus on the cross. Living for the glory of God must mean living for the glory of Christ crucified. Christ is the image of God. He is the sum of God's glory in human form. And his beauty shines most brightly at his darkest hour.

## Pressed by the Bible to Know One Thing

But we are driven to the same bloody place also by the question of a *single* passion. The Bible pushes us in this direction. For example, the apostle Paul said that his life and ministry were riveted on a single aim: "I decided to know nothing among you except Jesus Christ and him crucified" (1 Corinthians 2:2). That is astonishing, when you think of all the varied things Paul did, in fact, talk about. There must be a sense in which "Jesus Christ and him crucified" is the ground and sum of everything else he says. He is pushing us to see our lives with a single focus, and for the cross of Christ to be that focus.

You don't have to know a lot of things for your life to make a lasting difference in the world. But you do have to know the few great things that matter, perhaps just one, and then be willing to live for them and die for them. The people that make a durable difference in the world are not the people who have mastered many things, but who have been mastered by one great thing. If you want your life to count, if you want the ripple effect of the pebbles you drop to become waves that reach the ends of the earth and roll on into eternity, you don't need to have a high IQ. You don't have to have good looks or riches or come from a fine family or a fine school. Instead you have to know a few great, majestic, unchanging, obvious, simple, glorious things—or one great all-embracing thing—and be set on fire by them.

## A Tragedy in the Making

You may not be sure that you want your life to make a difference. Maybe you don't care very much whether you make a lasting difference for the sake of something great. You just want people to like you. If people would just like being around you, you'd be satisfied. Or if you could just have a good job with a good wife, or husband, and a couple of good kids and a nice car and long weekends and a few good friends, a fun retirement, and a quick and easy death, and no hell—if you could have all that (even without God)—you would be satisfied. That is a tragedy in the making. A wasted life.

## These Lives and Deaths Were No Tragedy

In April 2000, Ruby Eliason and Laura Edwards were killed in Cameroon, West Africa. Ruby was over eighty. Single all her life, she poured it out for one great thing: to make Jesus Christ known among the unreached, the poor, and the sick. Laura was a widow, a medical doctor, pushing eighty years old, and serving at Ruby's side in Cameroon. The brakes failed, the car went over a cliff, and they were both killed instantly. I asked my congregation: Was that a tragedy? Two lives, driven by one great passion, namely, to be spent in unheralded service to the perishing poor for the glory of Jesus Christ—even two decades after most of their American counterparts had retired to throw away their lives on trifles. No, that is not a tragedy. That is a glory. These lives were not wasted. And these lives were not lost. "Whoever loses his life for my sake and the gospel's will save it" (Mark 8:35).

## An American Tragedy: How Not to Finish Your One Life

I will tell you what a tragedy is. I will show you how to waste your life. Consider a story from the February 1998 edition of *Reader's Digest*, which tells about a couple who "took early retirement from their jobs in the Northeast five years ago when he was 59 and she was 51. Now they live in Punta Gorda, Florida, where they cruise on their 30 foot trawler, play softball and collect shells." At first, when I read it I thought it might be a joke. A spoof on the American Dream. But it wasn't. Tragically, this was the dream: Come to the end of your life—your one and only precious, God-given life—and let the last great work of your life, before you give an account to your Creator, be this: playing softball and collecting shells. Picture them before Christ at the great day of judgment: "Look, Lord. See my shells." *That* is a tragedy. And people today are spending billions of dollars to persuade you to embrace that tragic dream. Over against that, I put my protest: Don't buy it. Don't waste your life.

## Pretend I Am Your Father

As I write this, I am fifty-seven years old. As the months go by, I relate to more and more people who are young enough to be my sons and daughters. You may be in that category. I have four sons and one daughter. Few things, if any, fill me with more longing these months and years than the longing that my children not waste their lives on fatal success.

This longing transfers very easily to you, especially if you are in your twenties or thirties. I see you, as it were, like a son or a daughter, and in these pages I plead with you as a father—perhaps a father who loves you dearly, or the father you never had. Or the father who never had a vision for you like I have for you—and God has for you. Or the father who *has* a vision for you, but it's all about money and status. I look through these pages and see you as sons and daughters, and I plead with you: Desire that your life count for something great! Long for your life to have eternal significance. Want this! Don't coast through life without a passion.

## I Love the Vision of Louie Giglio

One of the inspirations behind this book was my participation in the conferences for college students and young adults called Passion '97, Passion '98, Passion '99, and now OneDay. Under Christ, the spark plug behind these worship and mission-mobilizing gatherings was Louie Giglio. He is calling young people to make a "268 Declaration." The number comes from Isaiah 26:8—"Yes, LORD, walking in the way of your laws, we wait for you; your name and renown are the desire of our hearts." The first statement of the "Declaration" says, "Because I was created by God and for His glory, I will magnify Him as I respond to His great love. My desire is to make knowing and enjoying God the passionate pursuit of my life."

This vision of life holds out to students and young adults so much more than the emptiness of mere success or the orgy of spring break. Here is not just a body, but a soul. Not just a soul, but a soul with a passion and a desire. Not just a desire for being liked or for playing softball or collecting shells. Here is a desire for something infinitely great and beautiful and valuable and satisfying—the name and the glory of God—"Your name and renown are the desire of our hearts."

This accords with everything I wrote in the last chapter and applies it to the upcoming generation. This is what I live to know and long to experience. This is virtually the mission statement of my life and the church I serve: "We exist to spread a passion for the supremacy of God in all things for the joy of all peoples through Jesus Christ." You don't have to say it like I say it or like Louie Giglio says it. But whatever you do, find the God-centered, Christ-exalting, Bible-saturated passion of your life, and find your way to say it and live for it and die for it. And you will make a difference that lasts. You will not waste your life.

## The Man Whose Single Passion Made All Else Rubbish

You will be like the apostle Paul, as we saw earlier, when he said that he wanted to know nothing but Jesus Christ and him crucified. Nobody had a more single-minded vision for his life than Paul did. He could say it in many different ways. He could say: "I do not account my life of any value nor as precious to myself, if only I may finish my course and the ministry that I received from the Lord Jesus, to testify to the gospel of the grace of God" (Acts 20:24). One thing mattered: "I will not waste my life! I will finish my course and finish it well. I will display the Gospel of the grace of God in all I do. I will run my race to the end."

Or he could say, "Whatever gain I had, I counted as loss for the sake of Christ. Indeed, I count everything as loss because of the surpassing worth of knowing Christ Jesus my Lord. For his sake I have suffered the loss of all things and count them as rubbish, in order that I may gain Christ" (Philippians 3:7–8). One thing matters: Know Christ, and gain Christ. Everything is rubbish in comparison to this.

What is the one passion of your life that makes everything else look like rubbish in comparison? Oh, that God would help me waken in you a single passion for a single great reality that would unleash you, and set you free from small dreams, and send you, for the glory of Christ, into all the spheres of secular life and to all the peoples of the earth.

## Christ Crucified, The Blazing Center of the Glory of God

Life is wasted if we do not grasp the glory of the cross, cherish it for the treasure that it is, and cleave to it as the highest price of every pleasure and the deepest comfort in every pain. What was once foolishness to us—a crucified God—must become our wisdom and our power and our only boast in this world.

God created us to live for his glory, and that God is most glorified in us when we are most satisfied in him. We magnify God's worth the most when *he* becomes our only boast. And I concluded that chapter with a claim that his glory can only be seen and savored by sinners through the glory of Jesus Christ. Any other approach to God is illusion or incineration. If we would make much of God, we must make much of Christ. His bloody death is the blazing center of the glory of God. If God is to be our boast, what he did and what he is in Christ must be our boast.

## The Shocking Summons to Boast in a Lynching Rope

In this regard, few verses in the Bible are more radical and sweeping and Christ-exalting than Galatians 6:14: "Far be it from me to boast except in the cross of our Lord Jesus Christ, by which the world has been crucified to me, and I to the world." Or to state it positively: Only boast in the cross of Jesus Christ. This is a single idea. A single goal for life. A single passion. Only boast in the cross. The word "boast" can be translated "exult in" or "rejoice in." Only exult in the cross of Christ. Only rejoice in the cross of Christ. Paul says, Let this be your single passion, your single boast and joy and exultation. If you understand me—and I hope you will before we are done—you will know why it does not contradict but confirms all I have written . . . when I pray for you, the reader, *May the one thing that you cherish, the one thing that you rejoice in and exult over, be the cross of Jesus Christ.*

For Paul to say that we should boast only in the cross of Christ is shocking for two reasons. One is that it's like saying: Boast only in the electric chair. Only exult in the gas chamber. Only rejoice in the lethal injection. Let your one boast and one joy and one exultation be the lynching rope. "May it never be that I would boast, except in the cross of our Lord Jesus Christ." No manner of execution that has ever been devised was more cruel and agonizing than to be nailed to a cross and hung up to die like a piece of meat. It was horrible. You would not have been able to watch it—not without screaming and pulling at your hair and tearing your clothes. You probably would have vomited. Let this, Paul says, be the one passion of your life. That is one thing that is shocking about his words.

The other is that he says this is to be the *only* boast of your life. The only joy. The only exultation. "Far be it from me to boast except in the cross of our Lord Jesus Christ, by which the world has been crucified to me, and I to the world." What does he mean by this? Can he be serious? No other boast? No other exultation? No other joy except the cross of Jesus?

What about the places where Paul himself uses the same word to talk about boasting or exulting in other things? For example, Romans 5:2: "We *rejoice* in hope of the glory of God." Romans 5:3–4: "Not only that, but we *rejoice* in our sufferings, knowing that suffering produces endurance, and endurance produces character, and character produces hope." Second Corinthians 12:9: "I will *boast* all the more gladly of my weaknesses, so that the power of Christ may rest upon me" First Thessalonians 2:19: "What is our hope or joy or crown of *boasting* before our Lord Jesus at his coming? Is it not you?"

## "Boast Only in This" Means "Let All Boasting Be Boasting in This"

So, if Paul can boast and exult and rejoice in all these things, what does Paul mean—that he would not "boast except in the cross of our Lord Jesus Christ"? Is that just double-talk? You exult in one thing, but say that you are exulting in another thing? No. There is a very profound reason for saying that all exultation, all rejoicing, all boasting in anything should be a rejoicing in the cross of Jesus Christ.

Paul means something that will change every part of your life. He means that, for the Christian, all other boasting should also be a boasting in the cross. All exultation in anything else should be exultation in the cross. If you exult in the hope of glory, you should be exulting in the cross of Christ. If you exult in tribulation because tribulation works hope, you should be exulting in the cross of Christ. If you exult in your weaknesses, or in the people of God, you should be exulting in the cross of Christ.

## Christ Bought Every Good Thing and Every Bad Thing that Turned for Good

Why is this the case? Because for redeemed sinners, every good thing—indeed every bad thing that God turns for good—was obtained for us by the cross of Christ. Apart from the death of Christ, sinners get nothing but judgment. Apart from the cross of Christ, there is only condemnation. Therefore everything that you enjoy in Christ—as a Christian, as a person who trusts Christ—is owing to the death of Christ. And all your rejoicing in all things should therefore be a rejoicing in the cross where all your blessings were purchased for you at the cost of the death of the Son of God, Jesus Christ.

One of the reasons we are not as Christ-centered and cross-saturated as we should be is that we have not realized that everything—everything good, and everything bad that God turns for the good of his redeemed children—was purchased by the death of Christ for us. We simply take life and breath and health and friends and everything for granted. We think it is ours by right. But the fact is that it is not ours by right. We are doubly undeserving of it.

1) We are *creatures*, and our Creator is not bound or obligated to give us anything—not life or health or anything. He gives, he takes, and he does us no injustice (Job 1:21).
2) And besides being creatures with no claim on our Creator, we are sinners. We have fallen short of his glory (Romans 3:23). We have ignored him and disobeyed him and failed to love him and trust him. The wrath of his justice is kindled against us. All we deserve from him is judgment (Romans 3:19). Therefore every breath we take, every time our heart beats, every day that the sun rises, every moment we see with our eyes or hear with our ears or speak with our mouths or walk with our legs is, for now, a free and undeserved gift to sinners who deserve only judgment.

## Welcomed Mercy or Mounting Wrath?

I say "for now" because if you refuse to see God in his gifts, they will turn out not to be gifts but High Court evidence of ingratitude. The Bible speaks of them first as "the riches of his kindness and forbearance and patience" that point us to repentance (Romans 2:4). But when we presume upon them and do not cherish God's grace in them, "Because of your hard and impenitent heart you are storing up wrath for yourself on the day of wrath when God's righteous judgment will be revealed" (Romans 2:5).

But for those who see the merciful hand of God in every breath they take and give credit where it is due, Jesus Christ will be seen and savored as the great Purchaser of every undeserved breath. Every heartbeat will be received as a gift from his hand.

## Deserving Nothing But Inheriting Everything—Why?

How then did he purchase them? Answer: by his blood. If I deserve nothing but condemnation because of my sin, but instead get life and breath in this age, and everlasting joy in the age to come, because Christ died for me, then everything good—and everything bad that God turns for good—must be the reward of his suffering (not my merit). This includes all that diversity that I wondered about at the beginning of this chapter. I asked, can work and leisure and relationships and eating and lovemaking and ministry all really flow from a single passion? Is there something deep enough and big enough and strong enough to hold all that together? Can sex and cars and work and war and changing diapers and doing taxes really have a God-exalting, soul-satisfying unity? Now we see that every experience in life is designed to magnify the cross of Christ. Or to say it another way, every good thing in life (or bad thing graciously turned for good) is meant to magnify Christ and him crucified.

## Did Christ Buy My Totaled Dodge?

So, for example, we totaled our old Dodge Spirit a few years ago, but nobody was hurt. And in that safety I exult. I glory in that. But why was nobody hurt? That was a gift to me and my family that none of us deserves. And it won't always be that way. But this time it was, and we didn't deserve it. We are sinners and by nature children of wrath, apart from Christ. So how did we come to have such a gift for our good? Answer: Christ died for our sins on the cross and took away the wrath of God from us and secured for us, even though we don't deserve it, God's omnipotent grace that works everything together for our good. So when I exult in our safety, I am exulting in the cross of Christ.

Then the insurance paid us for the car, and my wife Noël took that money and went to Iowa and bought a Chevy Lumina that was one year newer and drove it home in the snow. And I exult in the amazing grace of so much bounty. Just like that. You wreck your car. You come out unhurt. Insurance pays up. You get another one. And you move on almost as if nothing had happened. And in thanks I bow my head and exult in the untold mercies even of these little material things. Where do all these mercies come from? If you are a saved sinner, a believer in Jesus, they come through the cross. Apart from the cross, there is only judgment—patience and mercy for a season, but then, if spurned, all that mercy only serves to intensify judgment. Therefore every good thing in life, and every bad thing that God turns for good, is a blood-bought gift. And all boasting—all exultation—should be boasting in the cross.

Woe to me if I exult in any blessing of any kind at any time, unless my exulting is an exulting in the cross of Christ.

Another way to say this is that the design of the cross is the glory of Christ. The aim of God in the cross is that Christ would be honored. When Paul says in Galatians 6:14, "Far be it from me to boast except in the cross of our Lord Jesus Christ," he is saying that God's will is that the cross always be magnified—that Christ crucified always be our boast and exultation and joy and praise—that Christ get glory and thanks and honor for every good thing in our lives and every bad thing that God turns for good.

## Spreading a Passion for Christ Crucified—By Teaching

But now here's a question: If that is the aim of God in the death of Christ—namely, that "Christ crucified" be honored and glorified for all things—then *how* is Christ to get the glory he deserves? The answer is that this generation has to be taught that these things are so. Or to say it another way: The source of exultation in the cross of Christ is education about the cross of Christ.

That's my job. I am not alone, but I do embrace it for myself with a passion. This is what I believe the Lord called me to in 1966 when I lay sick with mono in the health center in Wheaton, Illinois. This is where it was all leading—God's mandate: So live and so study and so serve and so preach and so write that Jesus Christ, the crucified and risen God, be the only boast of this generation. And if this is my job, yours is the same, just in a different form: to live and speak in such a way that the worth of "Christ crucified" is seen and savored by more and more people. It will be costly for us as it was for him.

## The Only Place to Boast in the Cross Is on the Cross

If we desire that there be no boasting except in the cross, then we must live near the cross—indeed we must live on the cross. This is shocking. But this is what Galatians 6:14 says: "Far be it from me to boast except in the cross of our Lord Jesus Christ, *by which the world has been crucified to me, and I to the world.*" Boasting *in* the cross happens when you are *on* the cross. Is that not what Paul says? "The world has been crucified to me, and I [have been crucified] to the world." The world is dead to me, and I am dead to the world. Why? Because I have been crucified. We learn to boast in the cross and exult in the cross when we are on the cross. And until our selves are crucified there, our boast will be in ourselves.

But what does this mean? When did this happen? When were we crucified? The Bible gives the answer in Galatians 2:19-20: "I have been crucified with Christ. It is no longer I who live, but Christ who lives in me. And the life I now live in the flesh I live by faith in the Son of God, who loved me and gave himself for me." When Christ died, we died. The glorious meaning of the death of Christ is that when he died, all those who are his died in him. The death that he died for us all becomes our death when we are united to Christ by faith (Romans 6:5).

But you say, "Aren't I alive? I feel alive." Well, here is a need for education. We must learn what happened to us. We must be taught these things. That is why Galatians 2:20 and Galatians 6:14 are in the Bible. God is teaching us what happened to us, so that we can know ourselves, and know his way of working with us, and exult in him and in his Son and in the cross as we ought.

## Linking with the Death and Life of Christ Crucified

Consider Galatians 2:19-20 again. We will see that, yes, we are dead and, yes, we are alive. "I have been crucified with Christ [so I am dead]. It is no longer I who live, but Christ who lives in me. And the life I now live in the flesh [so, yes, I am alive, but it isn't the same "I" as the "I" who died] I live by faith in the Son of God, who loved me and gave himself for me." In other words, the "I" who lives is the new "I" of faith. The new creation lives. The believer lives. The old self died on the cross with Jesus.

You may ask, "What's the key for linking up with this reality? How can this be mine? How can I be among the dead who are alive with Christ and who see and savor and spread the glory of the cross?" The answer is implied in the words about *faith* in Galatians 2:20. "The life I now live . . . I live *by faith* in the Son of God." That is the link. God links you to his Son by faith. And when he does, there is a union with the Son of God so that his death becomes your death and his life becomes your life.

## Dying, Living, and Boasting in the Cross

Now let's take all that over to Galatians 6:14, and we will see how we come to live totally for the glory of Christ crucified. "Far be it from me to boast except in the cross of our Lord Jesus Christ, by which the world has been crucified to me, and I to the world." That is, don't boast in anything except in the cross. How shall we become so radically cross-exalting? How can we become the kind of people who trace all our joy back to joy in Christ and him crucified? Answer: The old self that loves to boast and exult and rejoice in other things died. By faith we are united to Christ. His death becomes the death of our self-exalting life. We are raised with him to newness of life. What lives is a new creature whose single passion is to exalt Christ and his cross.

To put it another way, when you put your trust in Christ, your bondage to the world and its overpowering lure is broken. You are a corpse to the world, and the world is a corpse to you. Or to put it positively, according to verse 15, you are a "new creation." The old "you" is dead. A new "you" is alive. And the new you is the you of faith. And what faith does is boast *not* in the world, but in Christ, especially Christ crucified.

This is how you become so cross-centered that you say with Paul, "I will not boast, except in the cross of our Lord Jesus Christ." The world is no longer our treasure. It's not the source of our life or our satisfaction or our joy. Christ is.

## Shall We Prize What He Presents or What It Portrays of Him?

But what about safety in the car accident? What about the insurance payment we received? Didn't I say I was happy about that? Isn't that worldly? So am I really dead to the world? Dead to insurance payments and new cars?

I pray that I am dead in the right way. I believe that I am. Not perfectly, I am sure, but in a real sense. How can this be? If I feel glad about safety or health or any good thing, and if these things are things of the world (which they are), then am I dead to the world? Yes, because being dead to the world does not mean having no feelings about the world (see 1 John 2:15; 1 Timothy 4:3). It means that every legitimate pleasure in the world becomes a blood-bought evidence of Christ's love, and an occasion of boasting in the cross. We are dead to insurance payments when the money is not what satisfies, but Christ crucified, the Giver, satisfies.

C. S. Lewis illustrates what I mean by an experience he had in a toolshed.

> I was standing today in the dark toolshed. The sun was shining outside and through the crack at the top of the door there came a

> sunbeam. From where I stood that beam of light, with the specks of dust floating in it, was the most striking thing in the place. Everything else was almost pitch-black. I was seeing the beam, not seeing things by it.
>
> Then I moved, so that the beam fell on my eyes. Instantly the whole previous picture vanished. I saw no toolshed, and (above all) no beam. Instead I saw, framed in the irregular cranny at the top of the door, green leaves moving on the branches of a tree outside and beyond that, ninety-odd million miles away, the sun. Looking along the beam, and looking at the beam are very different experiences.[1]

The sunbeams of blessing in our lives are bright in and of themselves. They also give light to the ground where we walk. But there is a higher purpose for these blessings. God means for us to do more than stand outside them and admire them for what they are. Even more, he means for us to walk into them and see the sun from which they come. If the beams are beautiful, the sun is even more beautiful. God's aim is not that we merely admire his gifts, but, even more, his glory.

## We Die to the Innocent World in the Blaze of Christ's Glory

Now the point is that the glory of Christ, manifest especially in his death and resurrection, is the glory above and behind every blessing we enjoy. He purchased everything that is good for us. His glory is where the quest of our affections must end. Everything else is a pointer—a parable of this beauty. When our hearts run back up along the beam of blessing to the source in the blazing glory of the cross, then the worldliness of the blessing is dead, and Christ crucified is everything.

## The Only God-Glorifying Life

This is no different than the goal of magnifying the glory of God. Christ is the glory of God. His blood-soaked cross is the blazing center of that glory. By it he bought for us every blessing—temporal and eternal. And we don't deserve any. He bought them all. Because of Christ's cross, God's elect are destined to be sons of God. Because of his cross, the wrath of God is taken away. Because of his cross all guilt is removed, and sins are forgiven, and perfect righteousness is imputed to us, and the love of God is poured out in our hearts by the Spirit, and we are being conformed to the image of Christ.

Therefore every enjoyment in this life and the next that is not idolatry is a tribute to the infinite value of the cross of Christ—the burning center of the glory of God. And thus a cross-centered, cross-exalting, cross-saturated life is a God-glorifying life—the *only* God-glorifying life. All others are wasted.

*For more from John Piper go to desiringgod.org*

# 3

# Can These Bones Live?

LOUIE GIGLIO

We follow a God without limits. Sometimes it's easy to forget that because we can dream some pretty big dreams and come to the table with some pretty high aspirations. But all of those dreams and all of those aspirations are only a pale reflection of the dreams and aspirations that live in the heart of God. Here's how the Apostle Paul would put it in Ephesians 3:20–21: "Now to him who is able to do immeasurably more than all we ask or imagine, according to his power that is at work within us, to him be glory in the church and in Christ Jesus throughout all generations, for ever and ever! Amen."

This is coming from a guy who saw God do some incredible things. He witnessed the dead raised and saw the blind gain sight. He saw pagans and idolaters become Jesus people. He experienced the worldwide spread of an upstart faith. And even with all that, here he erupts into the kind of statement that lets us know that all of that, and even anything else that he could potentially dream up, doesn't even capture the tip of the iceberg. God is a God of immeasurably more.

We've seen that play out in the life of Passion again and again. I remember sitting in 1996 in a conference of youth leaders that was held in the same building that fifteen years later would house a Passion gathering in Atlanta, Georgia. I was only there for one session, and the idea of Passion was still in its infancy. All we knew at that point was that God was on the move and He wanted to do something amazing in the eighteen to twenty million college students in this nation alone. Right in the middle of that one session, the leadership showed a video documenting some of what God was doing in 1996. Specifically, they showed stories of a student prayer movement that had been born in Wichita, Kansas, and then they transitioned into a segment chronicling how sixty thousand Korean students in Seoul signed a declaration committing at least one year of their lives to establish a church in a foreign country.

Now at that time, all our little team at Passion was trying to do was figure out how to host our first event in Austin, Texas. We didn't know if one hundred people or five hundred people would even show up. Then I saw this video of a stadium filled with university-aged people in South Korea, and my heart blew up inside me. I found myself paralyzed with amazement because I realized in that moment just how small my vision was. It's that way with all of us. I was wondering if there were one hundred students in this nation willing to spend a couple of days centered on Jesus and His Word, and God used this video to remind me that He is the God of immeasurably more.

I want to testify, based on my experience, that it's true. I believe that He is the God of immeasurably more than what you can ask or imagine. I also believe that's true not just in the context of some conference; it's true in the context of your life. The case study I want to hold up for you to see this truth comes from the book of Ezekiel.

The book of Ezekiel was written to a people in captivity. They were the people of God, but they had been scattered from their homeland because of their own foolishness. That's always how we get into captivity, isn't it? Whether we find ourselves captive in a relationship, in an addiction, in a pattern of behavior—whatever it is that has a grip on us, it's not because of someone else's decision or because circumstances just happened to land us there. It's always because of our own foolishness, and we are more foolish than we want to admit.

That's what happened to the people of God. Slowly, over time, they had forgotten who He was and because they did, they forgot who they were as His people. Because of their foolishness, they had been dragged off into captivity in foreign lands. But even then God intervened. He sent a voice:

> For I will take you out of the nations; I will gather you from all the countries and bring you back into your own land. I will sprinkle clean water on you, and you will be clean; I will cleanse you from all your impurities and from all your idols. I will give you a new heart and put a new spirit in you; I will remove from you your heart of stone and give you a heart of flesh. And I will put my Spirit in you and move you to follow my decrees and be careful to keep my laws. (Ezekiel 36:24–27)

That's what God does. He sends a voice to those in captivity not to say that He wants to improve some lives. Not to say that He wants His people to measure up to a standard. The voice comes and announces that God is going to intervene in the lives of those who have laid down in the midst of their own simplicity and foolishness, and He is going to give them new life.

Now maybe it's at this point that you might be thinking, *Not this captivity. Not in this life.* Maybe you want to believe it could be so; you really want to buy into this. But you've had one too many disappointments, one too many mistakes, experienced one too many setbacks, and you simply can't imagine that God could actually breathe new life into you. But let me remind you again that God is not confined by what you can imagine. He's not constrained by what you can think up. He's the God of immeasurably more.

Just in case the prophet Ezekiel, who originally heard these words, was thinking any of the same things as he was staring at a scattered people, God went on to give him a little object lesson in chapter 37:

> The hand of the LORD was on me, and he brought me out by the Spirit of the LORD and set me in the middle of a valley; it was full of bones. He led me back and forth among them, and I saw a great many bones on the floor of the valley, bones that were very dry. (vv. 1–2)

Can you think of a more desolate and lifeless place? Ezekiel finds himself in a valley littered with the bones of men and women. And these bones have been there for so long, and the valley is so dry, that they are brittle and hard. They crunch underneath his feet as he walks back and forth. Bones as far as the eye can see. *No way anything could live here.* Nothing but desolation. Can you imagine what the prophet thought about a place like that? Bones mean death has come and all that's left is the aftereffects. And that's just the kind of place you might find yourself in right now.

Ezekiel's valley represents the lowest and the darkest place of life—the place full of the hard and the brittle, the lifeless and the desolate. Maybe something lived in that place once, but that was a long time ago.

In this valley, to this prophet, the Lord came with a question: "Ezekiel, son of man, can these bones live?"

I like that about God. He seems to always be leaning into our lives with these questions that, of course, He already knows the answers to. The question He asked Ezekiel is meant to gauge our understanding of who He is. Ezekiel bites at the question, but he answers the right way: "Sovereign LORD, you alone know" (Ezekiel 37:3).

Very wise. As a matter of fact, that might be a wise way to answer any time God asks you a question. If we answer any other way, we are inevitably going to fall back on what we can dream, what we can know, and what we can imagine. But this God is the God of immeasurably more, so when He asks a question, the right answer is one that acknowledges the fact that no matter what we might see when we look at a valley of dry bones, it's certainly not the same thing that the God of immeasurably more sees.

Oh Sovereign Lord, You alone know.

When the Lord walks us into the desolate places of our lives—the addiction or the broken relationship, the job loss or the financial trouble, the disease or the anxiety, and He asks, "What about it? Can these dry bones live?" All He really wants you to say is, "Oh Sovereign Lord, only You know that." Then He'll respond, "Yes I do. And you better believe they can."

That's more or less what Jesus said in Mark 9 when He, too,

encountered a seemingly hopeless situation. In that chapter, Jesus rolled up on a scene of confusion involving His disciples, some religious leaders of the time, a hurting father, and a sick boy. All of the people there needed to have their expectations realigned to the God of immeasurably more:

> When they came to the other disciples, they saw a large crowd around them and the teachers of the law arguing with them. As soon as all the people saw Jesus, they were overwhelmed with wonder and ran to greet him.
>
> "What are you arguing with them about?" he asked.
>
> A man in the crowd answered, "Teacher, I brought you my son, who is possessed by a spirit that has robbed him of speech. Whenever it seizes him, it throws him to the ground. He foams at the mouth, gnashes his teeth and becomes rigid. I asked your disciples to drive out the spirit, but they could not."
>
> "You unbelieving generation," Jesus replied, "how long shall I stay with you? How long shall I put up with you? Bring the boy to me." (Mark 9:14–19)

We see someone in captivity in this passage, and we see a desperate father who has come to the followers of this man named Jesus to see if they could help. Maybe He heard stories about this man, stories about the things He could do, and he's hanging onto the thread of a hope that maybe, just maybe, Jesus can do something to change the situation. But to his disappointment, Jesus wasn't there. His followers were though, and that was better than nothing. So the disciples try and do what they had seen their teacher do countless times, but the situation didn't change. What made matters worse was that a group of the religious leaders of the day were gathering, too, and suddenly this boy and his hurting father became the center of a theological debate.

That's what Jesus rolls up on, and since it is, we can understand His frustration in verse 19: "You unbelieving generation. How long shall I put up with you?"

No one in the crowd really believes. Not the Pharisees, not the father, not even the disciples that had been with Jesus for some time. All of them were, in a sense, staring at this valley of dry bones and looking at it purely from their perception. Not one of them could imagine that any life could ever return there.

Jesus, though, decides to turn His attention to the father and digs in for a little more detail about the situation: "How long has he been like this?" (v. 21a). He asks. And the father answers, "From childhood. . . . It has often thrown him into fire or water to kill him. But if you can do anything, take pity on us and help us" (vv. 21b–22).

This is where we identify with the father. In our own valley, in the midst of our own dry bones, we look with doubt on Jesus. We forget that we don't worship a Jesus that exists according to our own expectations. We don't follow a Jesus who is limited by our dreams and thoughts. He is God in the flesh—the God of immeasurably more.

And that God turns the question back on the father: "If? Are you kidding me? Trust me, I can. The question isn't so much about whether I can; it's about whether you believe I can." That's when the father forgets himself. He loses his self-consciousness and exclaims one of the most honest prayers in the Bible: "I do believe; help me overcome my unbelief!" (v. 24).

I think God loves that prayer. In fact, I know He does, because the end of the story is life. It's a battle for sure, but in the end the boy stood up restored, released from captivity. Life instead of death.

Now that father's honest prayer sounds a lot like Ezekiel's response in the valley of dry bones. "Sovereign Lord, You alone know." In other words, I believe, or at least I want to believe. But I'm looking at this valley of death and for the life of me can't see a way in my wildest imagination that anything could ever live here. But You're God, and I'm not.

When we come to God like that, choosing to focus our attention on Him rather than on ourselves, that's when we're about to see something that defies the imagination. That's something God can work with. Back in the valley of dry bones, God was ready to do something that He alone knew about. At the heart of Passion is the belief that He wants to do it again—something immeasurably more in our lives and in the world, if we are indeed ready to see it.

Based on what happened next in that valley, I think we can see that this something that's immeasurably more is going to involve God doing three things. First of all, He's going to give the Word. In the valley, God told Ezekiel to speak the Word of God into the valley, and if we want to see something immeasurably more, we must be people of the Word. We must keep dwelling on and speaking the Word God has given to us.

When we do that, we come to see that the Word of God is not stale; it's living and active and sharper than a double-edged sword, and the central piece of God's Word is the gospel. Jesus is the living, breathing Word of God and has come to us to show us the God who is immeasurably more than we can imagine. If we want to see the dry bones live, then the place we must start is the same place Ezekiel did: with the Word.

The Word of God comes first, then comes the breath of God. That's what happened in the valley. Ezekiel was given the Word and he spoke it over the valley, and then something amazingly unfathomable began to happen. A bone zips into place here. A tendon forms there. The breath of God starts to move over the valley, and things start moving and shifting. It's something we've seen happen over and over again in the life of Passion, but even now it defies the imagination.

The Word of God goes out into seemingly hopeless situations. Someone sits under a teaching at an event or someone who has been with us goes back and speaks the Word in the apartment or their home, and immediately things start happening. Those things happen in places and situations that up to that point seemed devoid of life, but the breath of God begins to shuffle the pieces, and then what was dead becomes alive.

That's the third thing that happens. Life. Back in the valley, these bones become covered with skin, and they come to life again. Let's not miss this, because this fact resonates so deeply with who we are in this movement. Passion is not about religion. Passion is not about one ideology versus another ideology. It's not about how good we can be or how hard we can try. Passion is about the fact that sin didn't make us bad—sin made us dead. And when we were dead and hopeless and helpless, God had mercy on us. We were a valley of dry bones, but the Word of God came and God breathed new life into us. This happens because God does immeasurably more than we can imagine, time and time again.

If you're a Christian, that's exactly what happened to you, and the heart of Passion is to see that happen not just once, but in the entire world. When you look out over the landscape of the world today, you find yourself staring into a valley like Ezekiel did. You see twenty-seven million men, women, and children trapped in human slavery across the globe. You see people of every shape and size held captive by hopelessness and sin. You see disease and destruction running rampant, and you hear the voice of God saying to you, "Can these dry bones live?"

What we want to say as Passion is this: "Oh Sovereign Lord, You alone know." He does. And they can.

## Raised to Life by the Breath of a Living God

Let me take you back to the valley of bones in Ezekiel 37. God had asked a question to His prophet, "Can these bones live?" and Ezekiel had responded with the right answer: "Oh Sovereign Lord, You alone know." So the Lord takes it one step further, and what happens next changes everything:

> Then he said to me, "Prophesy to these bones and say to them, 'Dry bones, hear the word of the LORD! This is what the Sovereign LORD says to these bones: I will make breath enter you, and you will come to life. I will attach tendons to you and make flesh come upon you and cover you with skin; I will put breath in you, and you will come to life. Then you will know that I am the LORD.'" (Ezekiel 37:4–6)

So that's what Ezekiel did. He spoke the Word of the Lord over this lifeless valley: "I prophesied as I was commanded. And as I was prophesying, there was a noise, a rattling sound, and the bones came together, bone to bone" (v. 7). Talk about a freak-out moment!

Ezekiel is in a huge valley littered with dry bones, and then he starts talking to them. All of a sudden the sound begins, softly at first, but then growing to a deafening cracking noise as bones start colliding with other bones. The skulls jam onto spines and the toes join with the feet. Ankles snap onto legs as bones are now flying from all directions, and suddenly the prophet isn't looking at a valley of bones any longer; he's looking into a multitude of skeletons. Then, the Scripture says, tendons and skin grow on top of the skeletons, and appearing before Ezekiel are thousands and thousands of remade bodies (v. 8).

But they are remade bodies without breath, and the breath makes all the difference, doesn't it? See, it's possible to have all of your bones in order, have them attached with tendons, and have them covered with skin—to look completely normal—and yet be completely dead. Such is the case with us.

We might be serving in our church, listening to the right podcasts, know all the right information, or even come to a Passion event, and yet not have any breath of God in our bodies. We might be put together on the outside but be lacking the life inside. The breath makes all the difference.

Back to Ezekiel: "Then he said to me, 'Prophesy to the breath'" (v. 9a). In Hebrew, the word for *breath* here is *ruach*. This is the same word that we find in the very first verse of the Bible when in the beginning God created the heavens and the earth and His spirit, or *ruach*, was hovering over the waters. That's what Ezekiel was talking about—the life-giving, creation-bringing, power-endued breath of the living God: "Come . . . from the four winds and breathe into these slain, that they may live" (v. 9b). And if the scene wasn't crazy enough, imagine what happens next.

These bodies start breathing. Eyes start opening. People start looking around, and then they stand up on their feet. Any parent can identify with what that's like. A child suddenly starts discovering their arms and legs and eventually begins crawling. Then the crawling stops and they start standing up. Then they're back down. Then they're back up again. And eventually, over time, there comes the tipping point where a child becomes steady on their feet, and they suddenly realize what they were meant to do. That's this moment in the valley, because these dry bones—now filled with the breath of the life of God—are on their feet with purpose: "They came to life and stood upon their feet—a vast army" (v. 10).

That's a long way to come for a valley of dry bones. Death is now an army. Destruction and decay is now an army. Defeat is now an army. It's quite a turnaround, isn't it?

Now here's the thing about an army—it's a group that's been brought together and organized for a specific purpose. An army doesn't just hang out and mill around; an army is empowered with the interests of their home nation. These dry bones are pictured here as having not only received the breath of life, but divine purpose and meaning along with it. In other words, there's no disconnect from God breathing life and God launching into mission.

If you've been made alive in Christ, then you are enlisted whether you know it or not. One of the key parts of Passion is the recognition of that enlistment and making sure we understand that we have been raised up as a generation in order to be sent out. But sent out to do what? An army needs to have marching orders, right? Those orders are given to us as we begin to understand the heartbeat of Jesus. And Jesus understood His mission from God in terms of an Old Testament prophecy from the book of Isaiah.

Take a look with me at Isaiah 61:

> The Spirit of the Sovereign Lord is on me, because the Lord has anointed me to proclaim good news to the poor. He has sent me to bind up the brokenhearted, to proclaim freedom for the captives

> and release from darkness for the prisoners, to proclaim the year of the LORD's favor and the day of vengeance of our God, to comfort all who mourn, and provide for those who grieve in Zion—to bestow on them a crown of beauty instead of ashes, the oil of joy instead of mourning, and a garment of praise instead of a spirit of despair. They will be called oaks of righteousness, a planting of the LORD for the display of his splendor. (Isaiah 61:1–3)

Isaiah was, on the one hand, talking about himself, but he was also prophesying about another that would come—the Messiah who we now know is Jesus Christ. And about this one who would come Isaiah prophesied that the Spirit of God would be upon Him, and He would be empowered to bring freedom. That's really the essence of all these things—Jesus would preach the good news to the poor who were bound up in cyclical cycles of poverty. He would bind up the brokenhearted who were in chains of disappointment and sadness. He would provide release for all those who were held captive by the powers of darkness. Jesus is about bringing freedom; He's about exchanging beauty for ashes, mourning for gladness, and garments of praise instead of the spirit of despair.

Jesus saw this as His mission. We know He did because if you fast-forward to Luke 4, when Jesus finds Himself walking into His hometown of Nazareth, He looks to this passage to let everyone know just why He's showed up on the scene. Prior to this, Jesus had just spent forty days and forty nights in the desert being tempted by the devil in ways that we can only imagine, and He's emerged from that season of temptation with absolute, laser-like clarity on His mission and purpose. We pick up the story of what happened next in Luke 4:

> Jesus returned to Galilee in the power of the Spirit, and news about him spread through the whole countryside. He was teaching in their synagogues, and everyone praised him. He went to Nazareth, where he had been brought up, and on the Sabbath day he went into the synagogue, as was his custom. He stood up to read, and the scroll of the prophet Isaiah was handed to him. (vv. 14–17)

Do you get the picture here? God in human flesh is beginning His ministry, and He returns to His hometown. Standing there are the folks He grew up around and went to school with. There are people who knew Him and His family, and these people had heard all the rumors about the hometown boy making good. So He stands up in their midst, takes up the scroll, and starts reading. And you know what He reads? "The Spirit of the Lord is on me" (v. 18).

Then as he finishes reading that prophecy from Isaiah, He rolls up the scroll and announces with everyone's eyes glued on Him: "Today this scripture is fulfilled in your hearing" (v. 21). In other words, all the prophecy, all the hope, all the longing of a people—all of that just came into reality and fulfillment. Right then. Jesus closes the circle between everything God said He was going to do when He prophesied about a valley of dry bones, when He said the Spirit of God is going to exchange ashes for beauty and mourning with gladness. That is absolutely happening in the person of Jesus Christ. In Jesus Christ, we see the year of the Lord's favor.

Now here's where we fit in. We were the valley of dry bones. We were lifeless and without hope. We were the prisoners, the captives, the ashes, the mourning, those in darkness and despair. But just as God did in the valley of dry bones, He has swept into our midst, proclaimed His Word, and then breathed new life into us. We are the people of Isaiah 61 and Luke 4, and because we are, there's been a massive change of trajectory in our lives.

Our ashes have been exchanged. Our mourning has been reversed. Our darkness has been filled with light. And now we are called oaks of righteousness, a planting of the Lord for the display of His splendor. Just as the dry bones in Ezekiel's valley were formed into an army, so are we. Isaiah 61 tells us about our purpose if we keep reading:

> They will rebuild the ancient ruins and restore the places long devastated; they will renew the ruined cities that have been devastated for generations. Strangers will shepherd your flocks; foreigners will work your fields and vineyards. And you will be called priests of the LORD, you will be named ministers of our God. You will feed on the wealth of nations, and in their riches you will boast. Instead of your shame you will receive a double portion, and instead of disgrace you will rejoice in your inheritance. And so you will inherit a double portion in your land, and everlasting joy will be yours. For I, the LORD, love justice. . . . For as the soil makes the sprout come up and a garden causes seeds to grow, so the Sovereign LORD will make righteousness and praise spring up before all nations. (Isaiah 61:4–8a, 11)

This is what's happening *now.* It's what's happening in and through us. We no longer have to sit back, like the people of Nazareth before Jesus rolled up in the synagogue, and think to ourselves, *Maybe someday it's going to be the year of the Lord's favor. Maybe someday God is going to bring freedom. Maybe someday.*

The tomb is empty now. Death has been defeated now. The year of the Lord's favor is now. Jesus is alive, the Spirit has come, and we have the very breath of God's life in our lungs. We are the army of God, raised to life out of the valley of death, and we are joining Jesus in His mission. Because of that reality, everything is different, and I want to highlight four of those differences that are very near to the heart of Passion.

First of all, we have a different message. That message is pretty simple: I was dead and now I'm alive.

Let's not overcomplicate this. Our message isn't that we used to go to church and now we're really starting to get back into going again. It's not that our behavior has changed and now we're a little more moral than we used to be. It's not even saying to the world that the world is dead and needs to be made alive. The message is about you. And it's about me.

It's that I once was a stack of dry bones, but God has breathed new life in me and now I'm alive and I'm going to be alive forever.

Not only has our message changed, our identity has changed. Isaiah gets at this as well—we are an army. He says we are priests. We are the rebuilders of the devastation. We are the people of God, raised to new life in Jesus Christ.

Let's not overcomplicate this either, because we have the tendency to align ourselves with all different kinds of organizations and people. We like this teacher or that emphasis; we like this kind of worship or that purpose. In the end, we are the people of God. In all the ways imaginable, we once were not, and now we are.

Our witness has also been changed. That witness is our healed and healing wounds. This as much as anything shows what changes when we are brought from death to life. I remember at one of our events a young lady came up to one of our community group leaders and handed him a razor blade, as a visible symbol of the healing that the Lord is bringing to her. I have full confidence that the scars on her arm that were once a mark of death are going to be displayed someday as evidence of the life-giving power of God. That's the way it was for Jesus.

God didn't take away the holes in His hands and His side; the scars remained. But they were transformed from a mark of pain to a mark of victory. The same thing happens to us through the power of the Holy Spirit. We bear these marks of what once was so that we can show what now is.

Our message is changed. Our identity is changed. Our witness is changed. And now our freedom is changed. In the people of God we have been given freedom for the sake of freedom. If we miss this, then we'll start to think that Jesus brings us freedom for our betterment. But freedom begets freedom; it's a transference. Because Christ has set us free, we are to commit ourselves to the cause of bringing freedom to others. That's what we're after, and that's why we want to devote ourselves in this movement to seeing the freedom of Jesus spread to all corners and all arenas of the globe.

That means that we devote ourselves to the twenty-seven million people who are captives in some form of physical slavery or another all across the world. It means we fight on behalf of those who are enslaved around us to materialism and addiction. It means we proclaim the year of the Lord's favor not as an idea but as a reality—one that we are living right in the middle of.

The final thing that's changed is our worship, and I mean more than just singing a few songs. Worship is what happens when we give God His breath back. Though we were dead in our sins, God gave us His breath. His *ruach*. His *pneuma* (in the Greek). His life-giving Spirit. When we worship, we give it back, and we do that every moment of our lives.

Our entire lives are all about one singular legacy in light of what's changed because of Jesus. God made me an oak of righteousness, a planting of the Lord for the display of His splendor. My legacy is singular, and it is the glory of the One who gave me breath all over again. It's not about you. It's not about me. It's about the Giver of breath who made us alive when we were dead.

# 4

# The Captivated Mind

BETH MOORE

You have been set on this earth, at this hour, and in this generation to bring fame to the Lord Jesus Christ in your sphere of influence. And make no mistake: He has a specific way He wants you to bring Him that fame. The challenge and joy of following Christ is discovering what that looks like for each of us. But discernment does not fall to us by accident. God delivers it to us very purposely through a renewed mind.

Romans 12:2 says, "Do not conform any longer to the pattern of this world, but be transformed by the renewing of your mind. Then you will be able to test and approve what God's will is—his good, pleasing and perfect will." In order to know the specific way God wants us to bring Him fame, our minds must be renewed. For instance, with your natural mind you might be able to know you should go north. But only with the renewed mind could you, in spiritual terms, know that you should go north on Interstate 45, merge onto Interstate 75, and then connect with Interstate 35.

You and I aren't just looking for one of four general directions on a compass. As Ephesians 5:17 says, we're looking to "understand what the will of the Lord is" (ESV).

Now I can't imagine God caring whether we put mustard or ketchup on a burger, but he does concern himself with anything that affects our calling, the foreordained purpose He has for each of us on this planet. He has a personalized, specified will for you, and He communicates His will through unfolding revelation and the course of time to your—you guessed it—*renewed mind.*

Recently, I took a brain tour on the website of the Alzheimer's Association and was fascinated by what I learned.[1] Did you know that if you clench your fists and put them together, they will equal the approximate size of your brain? Your decision-making processes happen in the front of your brain. Isn't it interesting that, when we are trying really hard to make up our minds about something, we often instinctively start rubbing our foreheads? Yep, right where those decisions are being made. Your memory is held closest to your temples. Maybe you'll also notice that, when people are trying to remember something, they will put their fingers up to their temples. They are literally touching where God has stored the memory. That fascinates me.

In our three-pound brain, we have 100 billion neurons that can make 100 trillion connections. Every one of those neurons has something growing off of it that we're told looks like trees. I find that particularly amazing because Jesus says in Matthew 7:20 that trees are recognized by their fruit. Whatever happens in our minds will bear fruit in our lives.

Science is able to measure the brain. What is its weight? How is it sectioned? What is its circumference? But scientists cannot even begin to estimate the mind. Think about this and let a little awe wash over you: your brain completely encases and houses your mind, yet your mind is infinitely larger than your brain. There is no definitive way to measure it. How many things can we name that are bigger than the material they're embedded within? If we come up with an answer (like a computer chip, for instance), isn't it interesting that virtually every example would in some way imitate a brain?

It's important for you to know that God has placed within you the capacity for brilliance. You have a brilliant mind. A few years ago a young man named Derek Amato dove into the shallow end of a pool and sustained a serious blow to his head. Thankfully he was able to get up and walk away, with tests proving his brain was functioning normally. A few days later, while at a friend's house, he had the sudden urge to play the piano that was sitting in the den. Though he had no training whatsoever, he found he was not only able to play. He played like a concert pianist. Somehow his injury activated something in his brain. He is the only documented case of acquired sudden musical savant syndrome.

I once saw on a program called *60 Minutes* five people being interviewed that have something termed *autobiographical photographic memory.*[2] A random date could be thrown out to them, say July 21,1991, and many of them could say what color they were wearing, what they ate, and what they did that day. This thing encased within our skulls is mysterious indeed and, in every single one of us, it has the capacity for brilliance.

There is another side, however. The same mind that has the capacity for brilliance has a capacity for darkness beyond anything we have ever imagined. Henry Ward Beecher said, "There are materials enough in every man's mind to make a hell there." I stumbled on Job 21:6 recently and it stirred up significant wonder in me about the power of the mind. It says, "When I think about this, I am terrified; trembling seizes my body." Think about what he's saying: all Job had to do was *think* about something scary and his body started trembling. The imagination within us is so strong that it elicits a direct response from our physical bodies and can cause them to react as if we are participating in the real-time events of our imaginings.

I once heard someone describe the mind as "the awareness of consciousness, the ability to control what we do and to know what we are doing and why." You might read that sentence one more time to get its full implication. I think back upon the course of my life, the defeat I have lived in, and the things I have done and can remember so clearly at times asking myself, "What on earth am I doing? I don't even know why I am making this decision." Have you ever asked yourself something like that? Have you ever caught yourself doing something diametrically opposed to the person you really wanted to be? Ever asked in a state of complete bewilderment, "*What am I doing?*"

Knowing what you are doing and why is a sign of the renewed mind. We can see this clearly depicted in our Father. I love the wording of Jeremiah 29:11 in the King James Version. It says, "'For I know the thoughts that I think toward you,' says the LORD." The wonder of all wonders is that God, seated on His throne, is actively thinking thoughts toward us, and He knows the thoughts He is thinking about. We were created in His image, and part of what sets us apart from the animals is our intellect, to know what we are thinking and why. Renewing our minds is almost impossible if we are not able to zero in on what's going on in our heads. Created in His image and invaded by His Spirit if we're in Christ, we can—and if we're to be victorious we *must*—think about the thoughts we are thinking.

The skeptical among us might object to ingrained thoughts

being able to substantially change once they're deeply set in there. Yet that's what repentance means: to change my mind in such a way that it changes my actions. Even after years of destructive thought patterns, we can, in the power of the Spirit, have our minds completely changed. And our ability to discern and distinguish the will of God is dependent on it. You cannot think with your natural mind and hear the leadership of the Spirit. Our minds have to be renewed.

Now this part is really important: the renewed mind does not come about subconsciously. It is a battle. Behold the battle language of 2 Corinthians 10:3–5.

> For though we live in the world, we do not wage war as the world does. The weapons we fight with are not the weapons of the world. On the contrary, they have divine power to demolish strongholds. We demolish arguments and every pretension that sets itself up against the knowledge of God, and we take captive every thought to make it obedient to Christ.

Sometimes when we imagine what our lives would be like if we gave ourselves over fully to Christ, we fall into the same trap as Adam and Eve back in the garden of Eden. We decide that God is trying to cheat us and we would be freer out from under His control. But when we take our thoughts captive to obey Christ (which is another way of saying renewing our minds), it's not to cap them, diminish them, devalue them, or cut them off. It's to focus them, to give our lives direction, and to show us what we were placed on this earth to be and placed on this earth to do.

Think with me about the word *stronghold*. I lived with the malady my entire life long but did not have a clue of what it meant until I was well into adulthood. A stronghold is anything that gets a strong *hold* on your mind besides the wholeness of the Lord Jesus Christ and His Spirit. It is anything that gets a grip on you or mastery over you. And it is usually something that gets away from you and can easily lead into addiction. That's why every addiction is automatically a stronghold. It always involves a mental preoccupation.

Ephesians 4:19 voices the New Testament definition of an addictive stronghold. "Having lost all sensitivity, they have given themselves over to sensuality so as to indulge in every kind of impurity, with a continual lust for more." When we come face-to-face with our addiction, for most of us our first attempt is to manage it. To handle it. Keep it under control. But the nature of any kind of addictive behavior or thought pattern is the demand for more . . . and more . . . and more. If you were thinking it was just you, it's not. It's the nature of the addiction-prone human mind and body, for that matter. The addiction comes in, takes over, and gets a strong hold on us. In 2 Corinthians 10:5, it's called a "pretension" because it pretends to arch itself over us and have more power over us than God.

Let there be no question that Satan will also encourage and coax and tempt and comfort us into a stronghold. It may not be politically correct to talk about the Devil anymore, but you better know for a Biblical fact that he really does exist. He is the enemy of your soul. For every plan God has dreamed for you, Satan has a plot to destroy it. In 2 Timothy 2:26 Paul encourages Christians to repent so that they may "escape from the trap of the devil, who has taken them captive to do his will." It's eye-opening to realize that God has a will for my life and so does Satan. And both forces are continually yearning and calling for more: more and more of the Spirit of Christ (John 3:34) or more and more of the misery of bondage. That's why we will never be able to simply maintain what we have now. We either move toward more of Christ or more of our flesh.

I'm a student at heart. So I'm always asking questions. As I prepare to teach I try to imagine what questions are popping into the heads of my listeners. Now, if I were you right now, I would be asking, "Is it really possible to live in mental victory? What are the chances that I could actually live without strongholds attaching and exalting themselves over my thinking?" For the answer we don't need to look very far. You can split your Bible down the middle, let your eyes land on Psalm 119:133, and see for yourself.

> Direct my footsteps according to your word;
> let no sin rule over me.

You and I are not going to ascend into some mystical state of sinlessness while we still live in these bodies on this planet. We will be completely overtaken in His completeness, the imputed fully imparted, when we see the Lord Jesus Christ face-to-face. There is, however, an ongoing sanctification of our lives if we are willing to cooperate in the renewal of our minds.

Here is the reality. You are fully capable of living victoriously. There is more than enough power in Christ for us to walk without any kind of sin having dominion over us. Of course we all sin. That goes almost without saying, but here's the critical part that separates the victorious from the defeated: we can well be free of dominion sin, the kind that has a hold on us. The kind that gets exalted in our minds. The kind we keep making room for. The kind that makes itself at home in us. You and I want to be able to boldly confess what Paul says in 1 Corinthians 6:12, "I will not be mastered by anything." If there is anything that has dominion over you, except for the Holy Spirit, it has to go. It cannot stay or it will wreak havoc over you.

Renewing our minds requires a fight against destructive thought patterns, but it also requires a fight against distracting thought patterns. There are a million new ways to distract myself every day. I love my MacBook. Like you, I never stop checking my iPhone. And Twitter is like my best friend. With all of these distractions I am never forced to take the time to really think about anything. I brush over the surface of important things without really investing myself. But we will not be able to discern the will of God unless we focus ourselves on the will of God. To truly walk in the anointing of His Spirit and fulfill every plan He has dreamed up for you, you must be able to completely lock in on God Himself and let competing distractions go.

I've learned this the hard way: when God speaks He rarely yells. He often speaks in a small still voice and, if we had any idea the joy and insight and direction and intimacy with Him that we stand to gain, we'd be desperate to hear it.

Psalm 27:4 says, "One thing I ask of the Lord, this is what I seek: that I may dwell in the house of the Lord all the days of my life, to gaze upon the beauty of the Lord and to seek him in his temple." In these days of multitasking and abundant distractions there is one thing that should rise to the top. Some of the greatest minds in your generation may never bring the impact they could because their minds will never be renewed enough to be still and focused before God. Our God is a jealous God. He wants to be your one thing. We need the discipline in this undisciplined culture to shut ourselves off from every voice so we can hear and know the one thing.

After the shepherds left Mary, Joseph, and the baby Jesus alone in the stable, the Scripture says Mary thought about all that had happened and pondered it in her heart. *Ponder* is not a word that currently has a home in very many of our vocabularies, but look past the word and think about the concept. Everyone around Mary was amazed about all that was happening. Just take a look at the terminology in Luke 2:18. But Mary went beyond sheer amazement. She actually let it sink in. She thought it through. She let none of it be wasted on her.

There is plenty of amazement in our church culture: churches that are amazing, events that are amazing. Books. Blogs. Tools. Software. Downloads. Bible studies. Preachers. Teachers. Worship leaders. We have more than enough amazement. Where change will come, however, is not in the amazement but in thinking it through. Meditating on it. Letting it sink in. Pondering what God has done. What God has made known. What God has brought to pass. We move on to the next thing too fast. You can't hear a still small voice, a gentle whisper when you are moving 100 miles per hour. Counter to your surrounding culture and maybe as the only person you know doing it, take the time to stop, push pause, and think about what God has said.

As you think, a physiological reaction is happening in your brain. A chain reaction is firing off in those billions of neurons residing in your head. When you think the same way repeatedly, that chain reaction burns a path through those neurons. For example, if a woman looks at a man and thinks a certain thought about him, the next time she sees him she will most likely have that same thought. I'll throw out a stupid example to make the point so you'll know it doesn't have to involve attraction. Maybe she decides the first time she sees him that his ears are uneven. The next time she sees him, she stares harder at that same anomaly and, lo and behold, they're even worse than before. From then on, unless she changes her mind, she'll mostly see a pair of unmatched ears coming straight toward her every time he's within eyeshot. See what I'm saying? It burned a path of thinking in her brain. The more we repeat our thinking patterns, whether destructive or constructive, we not only hatchet a path through our brains, but we pave it as well, creating a thinking superhighway where the thinking becomes automatic.

Some of us have laid highways in our minds that have taken us places we never meant to go. We keep going back to those destructive places and we don't know why. It started with our thinking, and if we want to go to new places, they will start the very same way, right there with our thinking. We need to burn some new paths. Agreed? In Christ, you do have the power to decide how you will think. No one gets to take that from you.

I come from a background of abuse. It began with my earliest memory and happened on and off in my young life until I reached middle school. Naturally my mind was filled with devastation, bitterness, and resentment. It caused me to be the world's most foolish person in relationships and in big decisions. It occupied an enormous amount of my thinking: mental images of all that happened flashing through my mind, stuck on repeat. I would get so desperate I would cry out to God and say, "Lord, as of today, I'm never thinking about it again." Any chance you've ever said that to Him, too? But I always would. Then I learned what it meant to renew my mind.

I began to think new thoughts about an old thing.

And guess what happened. Its power and hold on my life began to wane. Then I began to get a genuine glimpse of God's redemption: that He could use me to reach out to other young women who had been through what I had been through.

I have heard people say these words over and over again: "I cannot change the way I feel." Oh, that may be true, but you can indeed change the way you think, and that will change the way you feel. We can know the thoughts we think. We can change our minds, and that will change our hearts.

1 Corinthians 2:9–10 says, "However, as it is written, 'No eye has seen, no ear has heard, no mind has conceived what God has prepared for those who love him,' but God has revealed it to us by his Spirit." If you give Him your mind, He'll blow your mind. He will never cease to astound you. As much capacity for brilliance as you have, when the Spirit of the Living God gets ahold of you, He will do more than your eyes have seen, more than your ears have ever heard, and more than your mind could ever make up. That is what God has prepared for those who love Him with all of their hearts and all of their souls and all of their minds.

*For more from Beth Moore go to lproof.org*

5

# Trembling at the Word of God

FRANCIS CHAN

Not everyone who reads these words will follow Jesus in the years ahead. It's easy to get excited about spiritual things from time to time. It's easy to make commitments or to think that the passion you feel in a given moment will carry you through the rest of your life. But let's be honest. Just because you're reading this book right now does not ensure that any of this is going to have a prolonged impact on your life. Maybe you are one of those people who will read about our amazing God and get stirred up about living passionately for Him, yet walk away and never do anything about it.

Or maybe you're one of those people who will die for this thing. You'll live for it. You'll wake up early and beg for His kingdom to come. Maybe you recognize that this life is all about following Jesus. You believe this so strongly that you can only assume everyone else is crazy for living their lives for this world and for the small things.

Or maybe you're one of those people for whom it doesn't matter what I say. It doesn't matter what anyone says. You're not going to change. You've already made up your mind. You've decided not to leave the ungodly relationship you're engaged in. You're not walking away from your addiction, no matter how many people warn you about it. You're not going to let go of the bitterness you've been clinging to. You don't care about experiencing God. You're so in love with your sin, it doesn't matter what anyone says to try to call you away from it.

In John 11, Jesus raised Lazarus from the dead. I mean, He literally took a corpse and brought it back to life! You would think that seeing a man raised from the dead would be all anyone would need to believe in Jesus. And some did. But some people saw this happen, then ran off to the Pharisees to fill them in so they could strategize about getting rid of Jesus.

As you read this passage, you're left thinking, *Really? You saw someone raised from the dead and you still don't believe? This Man proves that He has power over death, so you set out to kill Him* (John 11:53) *and kill the man He raised from the dead* (12:10–11) *in order to keep others from believing in Him?* That's insane. I don't know how else to say it.

Maybe you are one of those people who will come into contact with God through a book or a conference or a sermon or something, and you'll walk away unchanged because that's just where your heart is right now.

Or maybe you're the person that will read what I say and live passionately for Jesus. It's not about what I write. I could write something lame and confusing and you'd still get fired up! I could even write something completely blasphemous and it wouldn't hurt you because you'd call me out on it. You know God. You love Him. You love His word. So you weigh my words against His (Acts 17:11) and are passionate about following Him no matter who might try to lead you astray.

Perhaps you're someone who simply needs a good reminder. Peter said that in writing his letters he was "stirring up your sincere mind by way of reminder" (2 Peter 3:1). He's not trying to talk anyone into it. He knows he can't force anyone to love God. Instead, Peter is talking to people who love the Word of God. He talks about their "sincere mind" and says that what he wants to do is stir them up by reminding them. Maybe this is you. Maybe you need a reminder of what matters, of what God wants to do in and through your life, of what He has called you and prepared you to do.

•

I finally got a GPS. I'm probably the last person on earth to get one. But I just kept waiting for them to get cheaper until finally someone just gave me one. (That's what pastors do, by the way. You talk about something and how much you wish you had it as an illustration, and then someone buys it for you.) I'm excited to have a GPS, because I know I've wasted more gas money by driving around lost than I would have spent in purchasing one.

But the thing I love most about my GPS is how she (my GPS is female) deals with my mistakes. Sometimes she'll tell me to turn right, but I still miss it for some reason. I feel so bad. She told me clearly, but I was distracted or something so I messed up. But she never gets mad. All she says is: "Recalculating." That's it! She never says, "Why didn't you turn? Now I have to do all of this extra work!" I'm sitting there feeling bad. It's my fault. I'm the one who didn't turn when she told me to. And she just recalculates and directs me there by another route.

I love that voice. It's so forgiving, so full of grace. When she says, "Recalculating," what I hear is, "Francis, you made a wrong turn, but I'll get you there. Don't worry. It's going to take a little longer now, so be careful to listen to me next time. But I'll get you there."

That's really what the Holy Spirit has done with me my whole life. I've taken some wrong turns. And He says to me, "Recalculating. Don't worry. I'll still get you there. I'm still going to form you into the man I created you to be. It'll take a little bit longer now because you really screwed up this time. But don't worry. I still know how to get you there."

I hope you hear the Holy Spirit saying that to you when you've made a wrong turn, when you find that you're not where you thought you'd be in your walk with the Lord. *"Recalculating. Don't worry, I'll still get you there."* At some point, you have to listen. At some point, you have to trust that God's Word is trying to direct us to life. It's time to listen to the instructions God gives and ask yourself where you're going to go.

•

I read a verse the other day that literally brought me to tears. It was Isaiah 66:2. It says,

> This is the one to whom I will look:
> he who is humble and contrite in spirit
> and trembles at my word.

God says, "This is the person I'm going to look to: the one who's humble, the one who's contrite or broken over sin." This is God almighty! Who is the person He's looking for? Is it you? Stop reading for a moment and ask yourself: Do I match the description of the person to whom God is looking?

And here's the part that really crushed me. It's that last phrase: the one who "trembles at my word." When I read that I just started crying. "Oh, God, I've lost that. I don't see Your Word like that. I don't know if I was teaching it too much or just reading it too much or studying it in class or studying to put together a sermon. But somewhere along the line, I stopped trembling at Your Word. You're looking on this earth, looking for someone who trembles still, someone who hears Your Word and cries out, 'Wow! That came from God! I just read words sent to me from God almighty, from the great I AM!'"

When you view the Word of God like *that*, you realize how much you need to listen, how much you need to act. I want to beg you to read your Bible. But that's not all. I want to beg you to not just study the Bible, but to tremble at the very words of God. I have been praying for a people to rise up that would take the Bible literally and seriously.

I want to tremble the way Peter did. Peter literally trembled at the Word of God. Matthew 17 describes an incredible experience that Peter had:

> Jesus took with him Peter and James, and John his brother, and led them up a high mountain by themselves. And he was transfigured before them, and his face shone like the sun, and his clothes became white as light. And behold, there appeared to them Moses and Elijah, talking with him. And Peter said to Jesus, "Lord, it is good that we are here. If you wish, I will make three tents here, one for you and one for Moses and one for Elijah." He was still speaking when, behold, a bright cloud overshadowed

> them, and a voice from the cloud said, "This is my beloved Son, with whom I am well pleased; listen to him." When the disciples heard this, they fell on their faces and were terrified. But Jesus came and touched them, saying, "Rise, and have no fear." And when they lifted up their eyes, they saw no one but Jesus only. (vv. 1–8)

Can you imagine what it would have been like to stand on that mountain? Imagine you and two of your friends walking to the top of a mountain with someone you know, and then suddenly this guy's face starts shining like the sun. You'd be terrified! And then two beings come out of heaven and start talking to him! Can you imagine how your heart would be pounding at that point?

Peter spoke up: "This is great. Moses, Elijah, Jesus. Unbelievable! I'll build some tents for you." But before he could finish speaking a bright cloud came and overshadowed them. They knew what that bright cloud was. That was the glory cloud. Suddenly they were filled with reverence because they realized they were in the presence of God. And then a voice came out of the cloud.

A lot of times when we pray, we say, "Lord, speak to me." Do you know what you're asking? The voice of God? The passage says that the disciples, including Peter, who was normally so quick to speak, fell on their faces. Terrified. Shaking. Trembling. Why? Because they were hearing the Word of God. They knew it was God's voice speaking, and they trembled at His Word.

His word was, "This is my Son. I am so pleased with Him—listen to Him." Can you imagine the impact this would have had? And as they were lying on their faces, literally trembling, Jesus touched them and said, "Don't be afraid." When they looked up, everything was back to normal. The only person they saw was Jesus.

Put yourself on that mountaintop. You have just seen Jesus in His glory and heard the voice of God say, "Listen to Him. He's my Son." You're on your face trembling because the whole thing was so intense. And then you look up to see Jesus. What are you going to do? Are you ever going to look at Him in the same way? What if He tells you to do something? Are you going to do it? What if He tells you to "love one another"? If you had just experienced what Peter experienced, you'd be running to anyone you could find and saying, "I just heard the voice of God! He told me to listen to His Son, and His Son just told me to love you. Here's everything I have. It's yours. If there's ever anything I can do, just let me know. I'm going to do everything I can to love you because the voice of God told me to do this. Nothing matters more."

That's what it would look like to tremble at His Word. Yet we open our Bibles all the time, and we have to ask ourselves, "Does this have even a trace of this effect on my life?" We read, "You are the light of the world" (Matt. 5:14), and we think, *Oh, okay. Whatever. What's next?*

Imagine trembling at everything in your Bible! With every page you turn you maintain a sense that "I've just heard from the voice of God! I've got to listen! I've got to act!"

•

Much later in life, Peter returned to that experience. He described it like this:

> We did not follow cleverly devised myths when we made known to you the power and coming of our Lord Jesus Christ, but we were eyewitnesses of his majesty. For when he received honor and

> glory from God the Father, and the voice was borne to him by the Majestic Glory, "This is my beloved Son, with whom I am well pleased," we ourselves heard this very voice borne from heaven, for we were with him on the holy mountain. (2 Peter 1:16–18)

Peter assures us, "We didn't make this up. I stood on that mountain. I saw Jesus transfigured. I heard the voice of God. I fell on my face. You can believe what I'm telling you because I saw all of this firsthand."

But what I find most fascinating is the turn of logic in the next verses:

> And we have more fully confirmed the prophetic word, to which you will do well to pay attention as to a lamp shining in a dark place, until the day dawns and the morning star rises in your hearts, knowing this first of all, that no prophecy of Scripture comes from someone's own interpretation. For no prophecy was ever produced by the will of man, but men spoke from God as they were carried along by the Holy Spirit. (vv. 19–21)

Peter started by saying, "We didn't make this up—you can trust what I have told you because I am an eyewitness." But then he says, "There is something even more certain than this eyewitness experience I had: the Word of God. It wasn't invented by people; it was inspired by the Holy Spirit. Pay attention to it!"

When you pick up your Bible, you are actually holding something better than a voice coming out of a cloud on the top of a mountain.

In another place, Peter called this Word "living and abiding" and quoted Isaiah:

> "All flesh is like grass
> and all its glory like the flower of grass.
> The grass withers,
> and the flower falls,
> but the word of the Lord remains forever." (1 Peter 1:23–25)

When a flower first blooms, it's beautiful. It has a real glory. But give it time. A flower will always wilt. And Peter says that your body is like that. Give it time. Its glory will fade.

We put so much stock in our flesh and in the things that we can see. We have so much confidence in our physical abilities. But Peter warns us that we're no different than a blade of grass. We're going to wilt. But the Word of God—that will last forever.

What you read in the Bible today was true thousands of years ago when it was first written, it's true right now, and it will be true hundreds and thousands of years into the future. We can get so caught up in the way our bodies look, but Peter draws our attention to the Word of God and says, "This is what you need to take seriously."

In the next verses Peter tells us,

> So put away all malice and all deceit and hypocrisy and envy and all slander. Like newborn infants, long for the pure spiritual milk, that by it you may grow up into salvation—if indeed you have tasted that the Lord is good. (1 Peter 2:1–3)

I have been praying for a generation like this. A generation that craves the Word of God like a newborn infant craves milk. Do you fit this description? You open your Bible because your soul is crying out for it. You read everything it says and think, *Okay, I'd better do that. I don't care if no one around me obeys this verse; I'm going to do it because this is God's Word.* You're not taking your cue from what everyone else is doing, wondering if it's cool to read the Bible and obey it. When God speaks, you listen. You tremble. You obey.

More and more people are pointing out that what we call *church* in America is different than what the Bible calls *church*. It's easy enough to point this out, but we need to get beyond criticizing the church. What we really need are men and women who love the church, who are willing to *be* the church, who are ready to show the church something different. I know people like this. You look at their lives and you clearly see something different. Something biblical. Something inspiring.

When we founded Eternity Bible College, I remember teaching these students in class. They would begin raising their hands and asking us, "This is what you're teaching us in the classroom, but why doesn't your church operate this way?" At first, we would look at them and say, "You're young. You don't understand." But after a while, we started looking at what we were doing and realizing that some of the things they were saying were right. We couldn't just teach these students good theology in a classroom. We also had to model it in our churches.

So we began to challenge our students to put these things into practice, and we committed to modeling the Scriptures alongside them. We said, "Let's start becoming the church and becoming the body that Christ wanted. Let's start *really* loving each other to the point where what's mine is yours and we have a genuine unity. Let's forgive each other. Let's put up with each other and hang out with people we'd never hang out with."

It has been a beautiful thing. I long to see more and more

groups of Christians who are willing to read God's Word together and tremble.

•

What would it look like for you to read the Bible and tremble at the Word of God? Start with Peter's greeting in his second letter:

> Simeon Peter, a servant and apostle of Jesus Christ,
>
> To those who have obtained a faith of equal standing with ours by the righteousness of our God and Savior Jesus Christ . . . (2 Peter 1:1)

Peter wrote this letter to ordinary people. People like you and me. And he addressed them as "those who have obtained a faith of equal standing with ours." In essence, Peter looks at you and says, "Your faith and my faith are equal. We're on equal ground."

Do you tremble at that? Do you trust that? Can you believe that because God said it?

I really struggled with this for a long time. Maybe you struggle with it as well. Maybe you almost feel like you're a less-loved child. Wouldn't it be arrogant to put yourself on equal standing with Peter? Yet that's what the Scriptures teach.

One of my favorite verses is James 5:17, which includes the simple statement, "Elijah was a man just like us" (NIV). Are you kidding me? Elijah? Peter? These men had a faith that seems so untouchable. And yet the Scriptures say that my faith is of equal standing with theirs, that they were men just like me.

Why is this so hard to believe? It's almost like we think of

Peter as having the righteousness of Christ plus the righteousness of Peter. But that's not how it works: "For our sake he made him to be sin who knew no sin, so that in him we might become the righteousness of God" (2 Cor. 5:21). Peter's righteousness comes from God. My righteousness comes from God. The Spirit is not less available to me than He was to Peter. Jesus' life, death, and resurrection weren't more applicable to Peter than to myself.

If you struggle with this, you have to start believing what God is saying to you through Peter and stop believing that you're some sort of less-loved kid. This is the Word of God!

I struggled with this for so long, but I finally realized that I was looking at myself rather than looking at the cross. I was looking at my actions rather than looking at the love of Christ. This isn't about me or the thought that I might have screwed up worse than someone else. This is about the love of Christ. It's about the exchange that took place on the cross.

If we actually took God's Word seriously on this point—if we trembled at this Word—then we could actually live out the grace that Peter talks about in the next verse: "May grace and peace be multiplied to you in the knowledge of God and of Jesus our Lord" (2 Peter 1:2).

I've been trying to take the concept of grace seriously. A few years ago my oldest daughter came home with a test she had failed. That's not permissible in my house. There's no excuse. So when she showed me her test, she said, "What are you going to do?"

I told her, "We're going out to dinner. We're going to go to a movie and out for ice cream. I want you to experience grace." I said, "Look, Dad understands grace because Dad was really screwed up. Dad did so many things that were just ugly in God's sight. And God still fixed me. He repaired me and is working on me still. He blessed me with your mom and with you kids. I don't deserve any of this. That's what grace is. He gives me things I don't deserve. So I want you to experience this. I want you to see what it's like to be blessed beyond belief when you really should have been punished."

So that's what we did. We celebrated grace.

When my daughter came home from school the next day, she said, "I told my friends what you did." When I asked her what her friends said about it, she told me, "They wish you were their dad." I'm not a perfect father, but I love the thought that in this case my daughter experienced grace to the extent that her friends wanted me to be their dad.

Can you imagine if we actually trembled at God's Word through Peter here? What if the grace and peace that Peter talked about really multiplied in our lives? Maybe people would look at us and say, "Man, I wish I had your Dad."

Is anyone saying that about you? Is God's Word formed in your life in such a way that people see grace and peace exuding from your life and wish they had your God? Peter says that this comes to us through "the knowledge of God and of Jesus our Lord." It comes from knowing Him. From a relationship with Him. If we are close to God and tremble at His word, then these things will characterize our lives.

And then listen to what Peter says next: "His divine power has granted to us all things that pertain to life and godliness, through the knowledge of him who called us to his own glory and excellence" (2 Peter 1:3). Think about what Peter is saying. God has given us everything we need for life and godliness. You're equipped for everything God wants you to do. Do you believe that? Do you hear this truth as the very voice of God speaking to you?

This means that when you mess up, it's your own fault. God

has given you everything you need, so you can't put your sin off on anyone else. We have to stop making excuses for our sin. A while back a guy in my church was telling me about his struggle with pornography. He had been on a men's retreat, and a group of guys had agreed to hold him accountable. But he said to me, "I really feel like these guys let me down. They didn't hold me accountable. They forgot to check in with me for a couple of weeks, so I slipped right back into it." Really? It's their fault? God has given you everything that pertains to life and godliness, and you're going to blame your sin on someone else?

Whatever you've done, just confess it. Don't defend it. God says to you, "Confess your sin. Come to Me when you mess up. I'll forgive you. I'll cleanse you. If you're not walking with Me right now, it's because you chose not to. Just confess it."

Your web browser has a tab called "History" with a button that says "Clear All History." Maybe you know that button a little too well. You push that button and everything from the past is erased. I want to tell you that you can clear all history right now. It is truly a beautiful thing. Stop defending yourself. Stop explaining why it was so hard. Confess and God will cleanse you (1 John 1:9). He'll remove your sin from you as far as the east is from the west (Ps. 103:12).

Peter continues by saying that we have been given

> all things that pertain to life and godliness, through the knowledge of him who called us to his own glory and excellence, by which he has granted to us his precious and very great promises, so that through them you may become partakers of the divine nature, having escaped from the corruption that is in the world because of sinful desire. (2 Peter 1:3–4)

Here is another good point to tremble. God almighty has given you "precious and very great promises," and through these promises you may become "partakers of the divine nature." Do you tremble when God tells you that? Do you believe what God says about you right now? Do you believe that right now, as you read these words, you're no mere human being? If you have obtained this faith that Peter speaks about (v. 1), then you are a partaker of the divine nature.

You have to ask yourself how seriously you take His words. Do you believe that Jesus died for you? Do you believe He rose from the grave? Do you believe He's returning for you? Do you believe that He has put His very Spirit inside of you and that you share in the divine nature, that you have escaped the corruption that is in the world? Do you believe that you're not a normal human being? Hear the Word of God and tremble! Believe what He tells you! Do something about it!

•

Peter warns us:

> For if, after they have escaped the defilements of the world through the knowledge of our Lord and Savior Jesus Christ, they are again entangled in them and overcome, the last state has become worse for them than the first. For it would have been better for them never to have known the way of righteousness than after knowing it to turn back from the holy commandment delivered to them. What the true proverb says has happened to them: "The dog returns to its own vomit, and the sow, after washing herself, returns to wallow in the mire." (2 Peter 2:20–22)

This is a crazy passage. Peter is saying that if we're going to hear the Word of God and not do anything about it, it would have been better for us never to have heard it in the first place. If this is how you respond to God's Word, then you're in worse shape than when you started.

Some read this passage and think Peter is teaching that we can lose our salvation. He's not. Peter is actually not talking about those who were saved. Look closely. He's comparing these people to a pig. We can wash him off, Peter says, but what is he going to do? He'll head straight back to the mud. Or he compares them to a dog. When that dog throws up, he'll walk away from it for a while. It's disgusting. But then the dog wanders back and thinks, "Hmmm, that looks kind of good. I'm going to lick it back up."

What is Peter saying? He's saying a pig is still going to be a pig. It doesn't matter if you spray him off with a hose, he's going to walk right back into the mud. Unless his nature changes and becomes something other than a pig, he's not going to stay away from the mud.

My fear is that we are doing this with many of the people who attend our church services. We hose them off every week by putting them in an environment where they hear the truth. They enjoy this clean environment and think, *This is great! I'm not going to sin while I'm in here because everyone is cleaning me off and keeping an eye on me. Perfect.* But what do these people do the moment they're left alone? Straight back to the mud! Licking at the vomit! Why? Because a pig goes to the mud; a dog returns to his vomit. If there's no change on the inside, we're just hosing mud off of pigs.

If that sounds like you, hear what God says. It's worse for you now because you know the truth and you were hosed off for a while. What you need is not a bath but a new nature. The Bible gives you the promise of partaking in the divine nature. I'm not a pig anymore. The Bible says that I used to be a slave to sin but now I'm a slave to righteousness (Rom. 6). I'm still tempted. The temptation is always there. Things look attractive to us and we start heading back down that path. But now there's a struggle. Now there's a pull that keeps you from going down that path indefinitely. Why? Because you're not a pig anymore. Everything inside you screams out, *I can't go back to that mud! It looks tempting, but I have to walk away from it.* That is the new nature at work within you.

Take Peter's warning to heart. If you find yourself licking at vomit, rolling in the mud, is it possible that you were never changed? Could it be that you were never really baptized, you simply took a bath?

Maybe you're reading these words and there's a struggle in your soul because you know you've been heading down the wrong path. The pull is so strong, but you know you can't go down there. You've seen the mud for what it is. You recognize the wretched taste of vomit. You have a new master now. You are a slave of righteousness. Maybe you've been moving in the wrong direction, but I pray that you can hear the Spirit of God saying, "Recalculating. Don't worry. I'll still get you there. Let me get you back on track."

Paul asks a rhetorical question in Romans 2:4: "Do you presume on the riches of his kindness and forbearance and patience, not knowing that God's kindness is meant to lead you to repentance?" God has been so kind to you, just as He has been so kind with me. But do you realize that God's patience, His kindness, His constant "recalculating," is meant to lead you to repentance?

I don't know what is going on in your life right now. I don't know what excuses you've made for your anger, your lack of forgiveness, your lack of courage, your addictions, your immoral relationships. But right now I beg you to tremble at the word of God and realize that if the Holy Spirit is in you, if you have a new nature, you have power over those things. And if you don't believe that you have that new nature, then tremble at the Word of God and make that your first prayer: "God, I'm stuck here in this mud, and I don't want to be here. Give me a new nature. I want to be a partaker of the divine nature." God will forgive you and cleanse you of that.

But maybe you're that person who needs to be reminded that you have everything you need, everything that pertains to life and godliness. You are a partaker of divine nature, and you can live as a holy man or woman of God, as someone who trembles at His Word even if no one else around you lives this way. I pray that you experience the grace of God in a powerful way. Maybe you feel like you've been earning an F, but my prayer is that you will experience so much of God's grace that everyone around you says, "Wow. I wish I had your God."

*For more from Francis Chan go to francischan.org*

6

# No Funeral Today

LOUIE GIGLIO

Over the years people have asked, "What's Passion all about?" *Is it about the gatherings?* Well, we certainly do that. We gather people in domes, on campuses, in stadiums, in churches, both in the United States and around the world. *Is it about the music?* Yes, we do that, too. Worship ushers us into the presence of God and fuels us as we run to the world. And what a privilege to be an environment where we can write and sing songs that lift up the name of Jesus and give voice to the global Church. *Is it about the teaching?* No doubt. We are a theologically rooted movement and we've had great teachers join our tribe over the years—powerfully opening the Word of God and pointing us to Jesus.

But if you want to really know what Passion is all about, you've got to look to the place we've come back to again and again. When you do, you'll see what's behind the gatherings, the songs, and the teachings. It's the passage of Scripture that is at the heart of this movement, one that continues to both anchor our movement and shape our trajectory for the future. Our core rests in this confession: "Yes, Lord, walking in the way of your truth, we eagerly wait for you, for your name and renown are the desire of our souls" (Isaiah 26:8). This truth frames our journey and, we hope, becomes an anthem for a generation of what to live for and what matters most.

That's been our desire from the start—that a generation will rise up across the nation and around the world with their sights set on living to make one name famous. A generation convinced that there is *no other name* like the name of Jesus and *no one else like Him.* And, as a natural overflow of their affection for Him and His for them, a generation that lives with a determination to make that precious name of Jesus known to every person alive. This, my friends, is what Passion is all about. We want to inspire this generation (and those to come) to carry the name of Jesus to all people on earth. We want to join them in living out the truth of Isaiah 26:8, "Your name and renown are the desire of our souls." If you get that, and it resonates with your heart, then you get Passion.

Let me show you what it looks like in real life. It looks like this passage from Luke 7: "They all realized they were in a place of holy mystery, that God was at work among them. They were quietly worshipful—and then noisily grateful, calling out among themselves, 'God is back, looking to the needs of his people!'" And then the last line brings us to this result, "The news of Jesus spread all through the country" (vv. 16–17, msg).

Don't you love that? When we are together in worship as God's people, there should be a sense among us that because of His awesome presence (and I use the word *awesome* accurately and intentionally) and His work we are in a place of holy mystery.

Sometimes that holy awareness of His presence pushes us to our knees, and we are quietly worshipful. We are reflective and introspective. We're stunned and in awe, barely wanting to open our eyes to look around. Do you know this feeling? Have you been in moments like these where you just want to cover your face and stand in awe of Him?

But all of our worship doesn't have to be quiet. At times that place of holy mystery brings us to our feet and causes us to raise our voices as something inside our hearts explodes in noisy gratitude. We can't be silent or still. Not even a little. This is why Scripture says, "Shout for joy before the LORD" (Psalm 98:6). In fact, every time we get a glimpse into heaven in Scripture, something quite loud is going on. But whether it's quiet worship or noisy gratitude, the end result is the same—the news of Jesus spreads far and wide. It spreads to the workplaces and the homes of the world. It spreads among families and friends, in dorm rooms and in boardrooms. His name travels fast, carried by a countless multitude—those who have tasted and seen that the Lord is good. That's when we'll know that we really are a "268 Generation," a Jesus generation released by His love for us and unquenched in our desire to tell somebody what Jesus means to us. We'll know that the name and renown of Jesus really are the desire of our souls. But in order for that to happen, something has to first come alive inside of us.

That's what we see in the background of Luke 7. What triggers the spreading of the news of Jesus isn't an event or a conference; it's a funeral:

> Soon afterward, Jesus went to a town called Nain, and his disciples and a large crowd went along with him. As he approached the town gate, a dead person was being carried out—the only son

> of his mother, and she was a widow. And a large crowd from the town was with her. When the Lord saw her, his heart went out to her and he said, "Don't cry."
>
> Then he went up and touched the bier [coffin] they were carrying him on, and the bearers stood still. He said, "Young man, I say to you, get up!" The dead man sat up and began to talk, and Jesus gave him back to his mother.
>
> They were all filled with awe and praised God. "A great prophet has appeared among us," they said. "God has come to help his people." This news about Jesus spread throughout Judea and the surrounding country. (vv. 11–17)

Talk about a story that could have gone either way! Here is Jesus, just walking on His way, when He happens to enter this little town called Nain. As He does, He meets a funeral procession coming out of the town's gates. Most likely what Jesus encountered was a small collection of friends and family carrying a stretcher with poles with a body wrapped up in cloths on it. Because this was the son of a widow, this procession wouldn't be on its way to a fancy tomb, but more than likely, to a low-class burial place, far outside of town. The destination of this dead son's body was probably little more than a hole in the ground. In some cases when people were really poor, the bodies would be buried upright, just to save space.

Obviously, the mother was crying, and she wasn't just crying for her son. She was crying because of all this would mean for her. In addition to losing her son, she was already a widow, which means in all likelihood she was under a lot of financial pressure. She couldn't own property or a business. She was on thin ice in that day and time, and she was dealing with the fact that with her husband already gone and her son now dead, she had not only lost those closest to her but was probably going to end up begging for what she could to survive. She had a broken heart and a bleak future.

But, just at the right time, Jesus' path crossed hers.

As Jesus sizes up the situation, His heart bursts with compassion for her, and He immediately assures her, "Don't cry." Jesus feels her pain; He knows what this means. He knows she already has one strike against her and now she'll be out of luck, out of hope. And Jesus, though filled with tenderness for her, knows He has the power to do something about her misery. Without hesitation, He reaches for the stretcher and stops the procession in its tracks. Can you imagine what this must have looked like? A stranger busting into a grieving, solemn moment, grabbing the "coffin" of a young man He doesn't even know. Having placed his hand on the stretcher, He speaks to the dead, decomposing body and says: "Young man, I say to you, *get up!*" (emphasis mine)

I love that there's an exclamation point here in the text. Jesus was reaching with His power and authority into death and commanding that which was dead to be alive again. And Jesus wasn't just hoping something would happen—He knew He had the power to raise the dead. Instantly the young man sat up, most likely confused by his surroundings and unsure about the half-pained and half-amazed look on his mother's face. No one was sure what had just happened or what they should do. A dead man was breathing again. Their friend was alive!

No wonder they all fell silent, grasping for words. Yet they couldn't stay quiet forever; they had seen a miracle right before their eyes. Some shouted, while others were still. Some knelt low, while others leapt into the air. This is what happens when the Son of God is in your midst bringing those you love up from the grave.

You might shout, "Holy mystery!" at the top of your lungs and then fall to your knees with a shudder of awe.

The heads of those in the crowd were spinning. All of this happened in a matter of seconds. This young man was moments away from being forever shoveled into the ground. If Jesus had rolled up thirty minutes later, He would have missed the funeral. If the procession would have walked a tiny bit faster, they might have missed Him. There are hundreds upon hundreds of reasons why this encounter might not have happened, but it *did* happen, because Jesus showed up at just the right time.

He met these people right in the middle of their parade of death, and maybe that's what He's doing right now in your life.

There are all kinds of reasons why you shouldn't be reading this book right now. Your Kindle could have been low on power. The bookstore might have been out of copies. The person who gave it to you might have saved it for another occasion or handed it to someone else. Whatever the case may be, the same Jesus who—at just the right time—walked into the middle of that funeral procession in Nain, is walking into your life—at just the right time—too. And perhaps, given the intentionality of Jesus, the stretcher in Luke 7 is symbolic for you. Maybe there is something in your life that is carrying you straight out of town and to the grave.

Maybe that stretcher is a relationship that you've tried to justify every way possible, but in the end, you know it's carrying you to death, away from the purposes of God. Maybe that stretcher is a misunderstanding of who Jesus is; you thought He was someone who was nice and sweet and only wanted a little bit of your attention every now and then. You thought that having Jesus as your "personal Savior" meant that He exists to personally serve you and get you out of trouble. That kind of misunderstanding can lead you to death. Maybe you're not even alone on that stretcher. Perhaps some of the people you go to church with have the same understanding; all of you have some basic knowledge of who Jesus is but no real understanding of His radical love and grace and no real resolve to follow Him. That's a form of godliness, says the Scriptures, but you are denying the power that raised Jesus from the dead, and that basic knowledge is carrying you to death.

Maybe that stretcher is your sin. You are living in a pattern of rebellion that you know, if you're honest with yourself, is leading you out to a hole in the ground. The stretcher could be a wound—something that happened to you in the past and for years it's been festering and growing until now, and you find yourself spilling out bitterness, hatred, and resentment. That pain is leading you to death.

That stretcher of yours could be made of various things: shame, guilt, intellectualism, pride, jealousy, lust, anger, pain, disappointment, an idol—*anything*. But whatever it is, you're being carried out of town right now, and it's only a matter of moments until you're going to be put in the ground. That, in summary, is the essence of the enemy's plan for your life. It's pretty short and simple: Steal. Kill. Destroy. The enemy wants to bury you.

But even though the enemy might want to bury you, Jesus is in the habit of interrupting funerals. He intersected the one in Nain and several others during His stay on earth, and He can intersect yours with the power and the willingness to raise the dead.

In light of that, this story shows us at least three things. First of all, this story shows us something about *who* Jesus is. During this day and time, a religious leader would not go anywhere near a dead body. If they did, they would become ceremonially unclean. In fact, if you were a self-respecting religious person in that culture and you saw a funeral procession heading your way, you would cross to the other side of the road. The people that dealt with dead bodies in Jesus' day and age effectively gave up their ability to be considered clean before God. They lived on the fringes of the culture—the kind of people that everyone knew existed but no one would own up to knowing.

But Jesus stepped in. He wasn't just a rabbi. He wasn't just a teacher. He wasn't just a prophet. He was more, and because He was more, He acted outside of cultural norms and standards. Jesus is God, and as a result, He plays by His own rules. He's not worried about what He's "supposed" to do or not do. He was clear on His purpose and mission—to glorify the Father by raising the dead. He wasn't going to let any taboo tradition get in the way of that mission. That's really good news for you and me.

It's good news because the enemy might try and convince you that the miracle of life in Jesus is for everyone else except you. Not you—you're too far gone. You're too dead. You have done too much, lived too hard, and are now beyond hope. But Jesus isn't going to let any of that stand in His way. He will walk right up to your stretcher, touch the very thing that's carrying you to the grave, and speak the same words to you that He did to this boy: "Get up."

This story also tells us something about the gospel. The gospel, in the purest sense, is that Jesus raises the dead. That's the basic story. Jesus Christ was crucified at Calvary, giving up His life to atone for all the sin and wrong in our lives. The cross was where grace was on display, justice was done, and our case was pled before God. Jesus died in our place.

But three days later, Jesus was raised from the dead by the power of God to show that He beat death, hell, the darkness, the grave, sin, and all of its power. Jesus interrupted his own funeral by the power of His Father, and that's good news for us.

The gospel is about resurrection: First Jesus, and now us. Here's how Paul puts it in Ephesians 2:

> As for you, you were dead in your transgressions and sins, in which you used to live when you followed the ways of this world and of the ruler of the kingdom of the air, the spirit who is now at work in those who are disobedient. All of us also lived among them at one time, gratifying the cravings of our flesh and following its desires and thoughts. Like the rest, we were by nature deserving of wrath. But because of his great love for us, God, who is rich in mercy, made us alive with Christ even when we were dead in transgressions—it is by grace you have been saved. And God raised us up with Christ and seated us with him in the heavenly realms in Christ Jesus, in order that in the coming ages he might show the incomparable riches of his grace, expressed in his kindness to us in Christ Jesus. For it is by grace you have been saved, through faith—and this is not from yourselves, it is the gift of God—not by works, so that no one can boast. (vv. 1–9)

The gospel is so much more than a self-help message. Without Christ, we weren't bad. We weren't unchurched. We didn't need a little help. We were *dead*. And being dead is a huge problem. Dead people can't do a thing to help themselves. Not one thing. So the gospel begins with really bad news—all have sinned and can't do a single thing to improve their standing with God.

But the gospel ends with great news! Though the gospel begins with people who are spiritually dead because of the penalty and the power of sin, through Jesus, the spiritually dead are raised to life. The gospel isn't a message of how bad people become good; it's the power by which dead people come to life. It's not about Jesus making us better. The gospel is about our cold, dead hearts starting to beat again by the power of God.

In this story, Jesus shows us that power. He shows us that He can do what the law can't. He shows us that He will do what the religious leaders won't. He has the power and the willingness to step into the middle of the funeral procession and speak to the rotting corpse and command it to rise up. As followers of Jesus, we are the resurrected people. We are those for whom Christ has done what we could never do for ourselves. By faith alone, we trust in the death, burial, and resurrection of Jesus Christ, and when we do, God bursts into decomposing hearts and breathes new, everlasting life.

This sort of blows apart the idea that the gospel is solely about a decision that you might have made when you were younger, walked down an aisle, prayed a few lines of a prayer, and then were baptized in a later service. The gospel is about resurrection; it's about who you are trusting right now with your life and eternity. It's not a past-tense thing—it's a present reality.

By that I don't mean we get reborn in Christ again and again. Rather, our salvation is active as we continually trust Jesus to bring life to our mortal bodies day by day, minute by minute. It's not about what we did "way back when" that causes us to be sure of His salvation. It's about the grace He produces inside of us as we trust Him right now to give us life. The best kind of salvation is not the kind recorded in the annals of the church rolls, but the kind we are clinging to with our last breath—the kind that raises us to life and sustains that life until the end.

This story tells us something about Jesus. It tells us something about the gospel. And it tells us something about what happens next. Remember what happened at the end of the story? Think about the scene. It's a total turnaround from the way it started—a funeral procession centered on death has suddenly morphed into a celebration centered on life. This widow has gone from the depths of grief to the heights of joy. But the story doesn't end with the son chanting, "I'm alive! I'm alive! I'm alive!" It ends with something greater:

> They were all filled with awe and praised God. "A great prophet has appeared among us," they said. "God has come to help His people." This news about Jesus spread throughout Judea and the surrounding country. (Luke 7:16–17)

Now to be clear, God never left, but He had been awfully quiet for a long time. Like four hundred years long. There was no prophet, no word for the people, for century after century, all the way from Malachi to Matthew. But then Jesus burst onto the scene to interrupt a few funerals. When He did, the people remembered the old stories again, and it felt like the days of the past when God was moving in powerful ways in the midst of His people:

"God is back. God is back. God is back."

God is here, and He's looking after the needs of His people, and the news about Jesus—not about the resurrected boy—spread throughout the whole country. In other words, hope had come back around not just for one family, but for an entire nation. This resurrection wasn't just for the mother and the boy; this miracle was a match that would light up the landscape with the blazing fame of Jesus. That's the end result of what happens when a bunch of dead people start walking around again. The one who brings them back to life gets a lot of glory.

Don't make the mistake of thinking that your resurrection

ends with you. It doesn't. There's more at stake than what happens in your life. What's at stake is how God wants to raise up hope in a community, a nation, and the world, to the point where people look around and see what God is doing in you and, in astonished wonder, think to themselves, *God is back.*

I can recount so many moments throughout the history of Passion when we would be walking on a college campus somewhere in the world . . . places like the University of Virginia, Cal-Berkeley, Notre Dame, Duke, NYU, or The University of Sao Paulo. Each has its own uniqueness, but you find the same themes in each place. Huge sports fame or academic achievement, or both. Rich history, and social scenes galore. But if you study the faces, you often see thinly veiled loneliness, shattered confidence, bondage to things that tear our hearts apart, and spiritual cluelessness that leaves souls empty. And you wonder, where is the worship of Jesus and the offering of His Word that is paving the way for people to say, "God is back . . . here!"

A long time before this meeting in Nain, the prophet Isaiah talked about the work of God's Chosen One, Jesus Christ, like this:

> The Spirit of the Sovereign Lord is on me, because the Lord has anointed me to proclaim good news to the poor. He has sent me to bind up the brokenhearted, to proclaim freedom for the captives and release from darkness for the prisoners, to proclaim the year of the Lord's favor and the day of vengeance of our God, to comfort all who mourn, and provide for those who grieve in Zion—to bestow on them a crown of beauty instead of ashes, the oil of joy instead of mourning, and a garment of praise instead of a spirit of despair. They will be called oaks of righteousness, a planting of the Lord for the display of his splendor. (Isaiah 61:1–3)

This is what Jesus did in Nain, and it's what He's doing now. He intersects the lives of those who are brokenhearted, held captive by sin, guilt, and the pain of the past. He steps into that prison cell of death and proclaims freedom and life. He turns the mourning into joy; He turns the despair into praise. And He turns ashes into beauty.

It's interesting that the story in Luke 7 happened in the village of Nain—a village whose name literally means "beauty." Jesus stopped a funeral procession and walked up to a pile of ashes in the making and turned it into something beautiful.

Perhaps right now you're thinking that your whole life is just a pile of ashes. That's all you've got. You've got ashes of sin, ashes of wrong decisions, ashes of disappointment and pain, ashes of unmet expectations. The message of the gospel is that ashes, in the hands of Jesus, turn into beauty. Jesus loves to interrupt funerals. He's not put off by the stench of death. He will stretch out His hand, in all His love and power, and make that which is dead to live again. Can you hear it? Can you hear the voice of the One who raises the dead? Because He's calling:

> "Wake up, sleeper, rise from the dead, and Christ will shine on you." (Ephesians 5:14)

It's as if Jesus is saying, "There aren't going to be any funerals here today."

God wants to touch your life and use your life to raise up hope for your generation. And there's nothing more powerful than someone starting this chapter being carried out to death and hearing the voice of Jesus say, "It's time to rise up. It's time to wake up. It's time to rise from the dead." It's time to let Jesus Christ shine His light of truth and mercy and grace and healing on you, and for you to walk back into wherever it is that you came from, and for the people who know you best to stare at you in astonished wonder and say, "What happened to you?" Because in the end, nothing amplifies the message of Jesus' power and grace more than a corpse that was once decaying and helpless now pulsing with new life and beauty. Jesus is meeting you here right now. Let Him touch you and heal you and turn your funeral around.

# 7

# Passion for the Supremacy of God

JOHN PIPER

I want to begin by giving you some of the reasons I was so eager to be here at this Passion conference.

**My Mission in Life**

One of the great advantages of being in a pastor in one local church for many years is that over time the vision of the church and the vision of the pastor increasingly become one. A year ago our church produced a vision statement that goes like this: *We exist to spread a passion for the supremacy of God in all things for the joy of all peoples.* I can say without any hesitation that this is my life mission as well as the mission of our church.

So when I received the invitation, read about this conference, and saw the word "passion," and behind it the text of Isaiah 26:8 ("your name and your renown is the desire of our soul"), I was hooked.

I want to spread a passion for the supremacy of God in all

things for the joy of all of you and all the peoples of this world. So that is reason number one why I'm here.

**Glory to God**

Reason number two is that I want to be a little match set to the kindling of your joy. I want you to leave from this place thrilled and happy in God.

And the third reason is I want you to see from Scripture that both reason one and reason two are the same reason. They are one. That is, to spread a passion for the supremacy of God and to be happy in God are the same pursuit. Because *God is most glorified in you when you are most satisfied in him*—which is the sentence that I'll come back to again and again.

The songs that we've been singing and the thirst we've been expressing are ways of giving glory to God. Because the more we find our satisfaction in him, the more we drink deeply from him and eat at the banquet table—which he is—the more his worth and his all-sufficiency are magnified. This is the angle on the gospel that God showed me in '68, '69, and '70 as he was doing a work in my life. There is no competition between God's passion to be glorified and our passion to be satisfied, because they are one.

**Torching the Glacier**

Here's another way to say this third reason for why I'm at Passion: *I'm here to torch a glacier.* I have a picture in my mind that comes from Matthew 24. In Matthew 24:12, while looking at the end of the age, Jesus says, "Lawlessness will be multiplied and the love of many will grow cold." I'm scared to death of growing cold. I hate the thought that my love for God, or my love for people, would one day freeze over. Yet Jesus says "It's coming!" It's coming like a glacier across the world. So part of my expectation for the last days is that lawlessness will be multiplied and that the love of many will grow cold. Now that could be a very bleak description of the last days.

But if you keep reading in Matthew 24, verse 13 says, "But those who endure to the end will be saved"—so somebody is going to endure. And the next verse (14) says, "And this gospel of the kingdom"—the good news about King Jesus who we're spreading a passion for—"this gospel of the kingdom *will* be preached as a testimony to all the nations, and then the end will come."

Now put verse 12 alongside verse 14. "Lawlessness will be multiplied and the love of many will grow cold," but "this gospel of the kingdom"—of Christ's sovereign, saving rule—"will spread to all the nations and then the end will come." There is a tension between these two verses. The tension is that it will not be cold people who are going to take the gospel back to their campuses. It's not cold people who are going to get it to the unreached peoples of the world. How do I know that?

Let's back up a couple of verses, to verse 9, where we find a prophetic word that is very different. Jesus says, "They will deliver you up to tribulation and put you to death. You will be hated by all nations on my account." Now if that's true—if we will be delivered up to authorities in our missionary labor, if we will be killed, if we will be hated by every nation to which we will go—we know one thing that's clear: it isn't cold people who are delivering that message. It's white-hot worshippers of King Jesus who will get that done.

Therefore, what I see in verses 9–14 of Matthew 24 is that, as the end of the age draws near, there are going to be people who are getting ice cold and there are going to be people who are white-hot enough to lay down their lives for Jesus among all the peoples of the world.

So my ministry at my church, and my arrival here, is to torch a glacier.

I gave this image one time in my church and a little girl, about 7 years old, came up to me after the service—I encourage the children in my church to draw my sermons—and she said, "Here's what I saw." She had drawn a marvelous glacier with Minneapolis written on it. It also had a little stick man holding up a torch, and there was a hole in the glacier, at the top. Over it was a lot of sunshine, coming down through the hole.

Now here is my eschatology in a nutshell: If you wonder what your campus is going to look like when Jesus comes, or what Austin or Minneapolis, or wherever you're from, is going to look like, here it is: the glacier is moving, and a lot of people are growing cold towards God, but there is nothing in the Bible about the end times that says Bethlehem Baptist Church, or even "Minneapolis," or the University of Texas at Austin, has to be under that glacier. Nothing! If there are enough people with torches lit white-hot for God, torching the glacier, a big hole can be opened up over your campus, over your local church, and even over your city. And that's why I'm here: I want to lift my torch.

Charles Spurgeon, a famous preacher in London over hundred years ago, would say, "People come to watch me burn." They came to take their flickering little torch and stick it in his torch and go out and burn for Jesus another week. I would be thrilled if you brought a flickering torch here today and put it in my fire. That's why I'm here.

**Foundation First, Then Application**

There is a foundation for what I want to do. My task first is to talk about living for the glory of God, having a passion for the glory of God. I have two parts in mind here. First is foundation, and second is application.

The foundation is this: Your passion for the supremacy of God in all things is based squarely on God's passion for the supremacy of God in all things. Your God-centeredness—if it's going to endure—has to be rooted in God's God-centeredness. If you want God to be supreme in your life, you have to see, and believe, and love the truth that God is supreme in the life of God. If you want God to be your treasure—as we've sung about here at Passion—so that you value God more than anything, you have to see and believe that God's greatest treasure is God, that he treasures himself more than he treasures anything. We may not withhold from God the highest pleasure in the universe, namely, the worship of God. That's foundation; that's what I want to address in part one.

And then in part two, I want to talk about your pursuit of joy in God, and that this pursuit is necessarily implied in God's pursuit of his glory in your life.

## Part One: God's Passion for His Glory

Let me begin with a little story. I spoke at my *alma mater*, Wheaton College, several years ago. It was my first chance to speak in the big, chandeliered, blue, beautiful chapel. I stood up and said, "The chief end of God is to glorify God and enjoy him forever." And all my friends who were up in the balcony thought, "Oh no, he blew it on his first chance at his own alma mater to speak to these students. He comes back after 20 years, and he misquotes the Westminster Catechism right off the bat saying, 'The chief end of God' instead of 'The chief end of man.'" And to their great relief, I went on to say that

I really meant what I said. I hadn't misspoken. And I really mean it now: *the chief end of God is to glorify God and enjoy himself forever.*

I grew up in the home of an evangelist. My dad, Bill Piper, taught me from an early age 1 Corinthians 10:31: "Whatever you do, whether you eat or whether you drink, do everything to the glory of God." But I never heard anybody say that God does everything to the glory of God. And that the root of my living for the glory of God is that God lives for the glory of God.

I had never seen a child bring home a Sunday School paper that said, "God loves himself more than he loves you, and therein lies the only hope that he might love you, unworthy as you are." Most of us grew up in homes, and in churches, where we got excited about being Christians to the degree that we thought God was excited about us, not to the degree that we got excited about a God-centered God.

It's very easy in a man-centered world, where self-esteem is the highest value, to be a Christian to the degree that it buttresses what you would've done anyway, without God. Who wouldn't be a Christian? Well, you're not truly a born-again Christian if you only love what you would've loved without being confronted with the beauty of a God-centered God. If God is only a means to your self-advancement and exaltation—rather than your seeing in him something infinitely glorious, as a God consumed with the manifestation of his glory—then you need to check your conversion. So this is a big reality check. Very few people have ever said to me, or shown me what I've now seen in the Bible, that God chose me for his glory.

I remember teaching a class on Ephesians 1 in January of 1976 in what we called "Interim" at Bethel College in those days, and working my way systematically through the first fourteen verses of Ephesians and having my mind boggled again. Because three times—in verses 6, 12, and 14—Paul says that God chose us in Jesus before the foundation of the world and he predestined us to be his sons *to the praise of the glory of his grace.*

He chose you. Why? That his glory and grace might be praised and magnified. Your salvation is to glorify God. Your election is to glorify God. Your regeneration was to glorify God. Your justification was for the glory of God. Your sanctification is for the glory of God. And one day your glorification will be an absorbance into the glory of God.

**You were created for the glory of God.** Isaiah 43:6: "Bring my sons from afar, and my daughters from the ends of the earth; everyone whom I created *for my glory.*"

**God rescued his people Israel from Egypt for his glory.** Psalm 106:7: "Our fathers, when they were in Egypt, did not consider your ways or your wonderful works. They rebelled against you at the Red Sea. Yet you saved them *for your name's sake*, that you might make known your power and your glory."

In other words, he split the Red Sea and saved his rebellious people, so that he might make known his mighty power. And it spread all the way to Jericho and saved a prostitute, so that when the Israelites came there and were ready to blow the trumpets, she had already been born again, because she said, "We heard your name and your renown." And one woman and her family believed in a God-centered God and escaped destruction.

**God had mercy on Israel in the wilderness for his glory.** God spared Israel in the wilderness over and over again. "The house of Israel rebelled against me in the wilderness," Ezekiel says, quoting God, "and I thought I would pour out my wrath, but I acted for the sake of my name lest it be profaned among the nations." And then finally God sends them into judgment in Babylon, and after

70 years, mercy warms to them. He will not divorce his covenant bride, and he brings them back. But why?

What's the motive rooted in God's heart? Listen to it from Isaiah 48: "*For my name's sake* I defer my anger, *for the sake of my praise* I restrain it for you, that I may not cut you off. Behold, I have refined you, but not like silver; I have tried you in the furnace of affliction. *For my own sake, for my own sake*, I do it, for how should *my name* be profaned? *My glory* I will not give to another." That's a God-centered motive for mercy.

**Jesus came and died for God's glory.** Jesus came into the world for what reason? O how many times we have quoted John 3:16. And it is gloriously true. And before this chapter is finished, I hope you'll see that this emphasis (God's glory) and the emphasis you've known for a long time probably (your joy) are not at odds.

But why did Jesus come? According to Romans 15:8, he came for this reason: "Christ became a servant to the circumcision to show God's truthfulness, in order to confirm the promises given to the patriarchs, and in order that the Gentiles might *glorify God* for his mercy." Jesus came to earth, became fully human, and died so that you would give glory to his Father for mercy. He came for his Father's sake. That's the main reason why he came, for his Father's glory. And his glory reaches its apex in the overflow of mercy.

Listen to this word from Romans 3:25: "God put Christ forward as a propitiation by his blood to demonstrate God's righteousness. It was to prove at the present time that he himself is righteous." That's why he died. He died to vindicate the righteousness of God who had passed over sins like David's adultery and murder.

Did it ever trouble you that God just passed over King David's adultery, and David just went on being king? Well, it troubled Paul to the depths of his being that God is not righteous to pass over sins. And it wasn't just David. There were thousands of saints in the Old Testament, and today, whose sins God simply forgets and passes over. And Paul cried out, "How can you be God and do that? How can you be righteous and do that? How can you be just and do that? How can you be worthy of worship and do that?" If any judge in Austin did that—if he acquitted a guilty child-abuser, a rapist, a murderer—he'd be off the bench in a minute. And yet God does it every day, so we might ask, "What kind of God are you?"

The cross is the solution to a mega-theological problem, namely, *How can God be God and forgive sins?* Jesus came to vindicate God in the saving of people like you and me. Salvation is a grandly and gloriously God-centered thing.

**Jesus is returning to get glory.** Why is he coming again? Jesus is coming, And let me tell you why he is coming and what you can do when he comes, so that you'll be ready and do it. 2 Thessalonians 1:9: "Those who do not obey the gospel will suffer the punishment of eternal destruction and exclusion from the presence of the Lord and from the glory of his might, when *he comes on that day to be glorified in his saints and to be marveled at in all who have believed.*" You see those two things? He is coming to be glorified (magnified) in his saints, and to be marveled at. If you don't get started on that now, you won't be able to do it when he comes.

This conference exists to light a fire in your bones and ignite a fire in your minds and in your hearts to get you ready to meet King Jesus, so that you can continue throughout all eternity doing what he created you to do, namely, to marvel at him and magnify him.

**Magnify God Like a Telescope**

So magnify Jesus by marveling at him, but don't magnify him like a microscope. You know the difference between two kinds of magnification, don't you? There's telescope magnification and microscope magnification, and it's blasphemy to magnify God like a microscope.

To magnify God like a microscope is to take something tiny and make it look bigger than it is. If you try to do that to God, you blaspheme. But a telescope puts its lens on unimaginable expanses of greatness and tries simply to help them look more like what they are. That's what a telescope is for.

*Twinkle, twinkle, little star*—we look up in the sky at night, and they look like mere pin-points. But as you know, that's not what they are. They are big. Really, really big. And they are hot! And we wouldn't have much of a clue about that except that once upon a time somebody invented a telescope. And astronomers put their eye to it and did calculations and thought, "It's bigger than the earth, millions of times bigger than the earth."

That's the way God is. Your life exists to telescope God's glory to your campus. That's a big calling. That's where we're headed in Part Two.

**If God Is God-Centered, How Can He Be Loving?**

Here's the key question to end Part One, because I can feel an objection rising at this point. For twenty years I've been teaching this truth that God is a God-centered God and that his God-centeredness is the root of my God-centeredness, and at this point the question begins to rise: "This does not sound loving, because the Bible says in 1 Corinthians 13:5, 'Love seeks not its own.' And you're telling us now that God spends *all* of his time seeking his own. So either God is not loving, or you're a liar." And that's a big problem. So let me try to answer how it is that God is loving in seeking his own self-exaltation.

**Help from C. S. Lewis**

I found the key in C. S. Lewis. If any of you have read *Desiring God* (Multnomah Books, 1986, 1995, 2003, 2011), then you remember this quote. Lewis was a pagan until his late-20s, and he hated what he thought was God's vanity. He said that every time he read the words in the Psalms, "Praise the Lord, Praise the Lord"—and he knew Christian doctrine, that the Psalms were God-inspired—he knew that it was really God saying, "Praise me, Praise me" and it sounded like, he thought, "an old woman seeking compliments." That's a quote from Lewis's *Reflections on the Psalms.* And then suddenly God came into Lewis's life. And this is what he wrote:

> The most obvious fact about praise, whether of God or anything, strangely escaped me. I thought of it in terms of compliment, approval, giving of honor. I had never noticed that all enjoyment spontaneously overflows in praise, unless sometimes we bring shyness in to check it. The world rings with praise: lovers praising their mistresses, readers their favorite poets, walkers praising the countryside, players praising their favorite games, praise of weather, wines, dishes, actors, horses, colleges, countries, historical personages, children, flowers, mountains, rare stamps, rare beetles, even sometimes politicians and scholars. My whole more general difficulty with the praise of God depended on my absurdly denying to us, as regards the supremely valuable, what we delight to do—even what we cannot help doing—with regard to everything else we value.

And then here comes the key sentences:

> I think we delight to praise what we enjoy because the joy is not complete until it is expressed. It is not out of compliment that lovers keep on telling one another how beautiful they are. The delight is incomplete until it is expressed.

That was the key for me that unlocked how God can be both loving and self-exalting in everything he does. Let me put the pieces together for you.

**The Answer to the Question**

If God is to love you, what must he give you? He must give you what is best for you. And the best thing in all the universe is God. If he were to give you all health, the best job, the best spouse, the best computer, the best vacations, and the best success in any realm, and yet withhold himself, then he would amount in the end to hating you. But if he gives you himself, even if nothing besides, he loves you infinitely.

We must have God for our enjoyment if God is to be loving to us. Now Lewis has said that if God gives you himself to enjoy for all eternity, that joy will not come to consummation until you express it in praise. Therefore, for God to love you fully, he cannot be indifferent to whether you bring your joy to consummation through praise or not. Therefore, God must seek our praise if we are to be loved by him.

Let me run that by you one more time. That's the essence of my life message. And I believe it's at the heart of the heart of the Bible: To love you, God must give you what is best for you. God is what is best for you. "In your presence in fullness of joy; at your right hand are pleasures evermore" (Psalm 16:11). God gives himself to us for our pleasure. But Lewis has shown us that unless those pleasures find expression in praise to God, the pleasures are restricted. And therefore, God, not wanting to restrict your pleasure in any way, says, "Praise me. In everything you do, praise me. In everything you do, exalt me. In everything you do, have a passion for my supremacy"—which simply means that God's passion to be glorified and your passion to be satisfied are not at odds. They come together. *God is most glorified in you when you are most satisfied in him.*

Now that's the end of Part One. Let me tell you where we're going in Part Two. If this is true, that God is most glorified in you when you are most satisfied in him—and therefore, there is no tension or contradiction between your satisfaction in him and his glorification in you—then the vocation of your life is to pursue your pleasure. I call it *Christian Hedonism*, and I want to talk about how you do that and why it will transform your relationships, your campuses, your worship, and your eternity.

## Part Two: Our Passion for the Glory of God

Part One was in an attempt to torch the glacier and to spread a passion for the supremacy of God in all things for the joy of all peoples. I hope I've sufficiently made the point that God does everything he does for the glory of his name. God magnifies God. The most passionate heart in all the universe for God is God's heart. That's the main point. This Passion conference, as I understand it, is about God's passion for God. Everything he does, from creation to consummation, he does with a view to displaying and upholding the glory of his name.

**God's God-Centeredness Is Not Unloving**

The second point from Part One was that this is not unloving. The reason it is not unloving for God to exalt himself in this way is because knowing God, and being swept up into the praises of God, is what satisfies the human soul. We saw in Psalm 16:11 that in God's presence is fullness of joy, and at his right hand are pleasures forevermore. Therefore, if God's exalting himself—to the degree that we can see him for who he is—satisfies our souls, then God is the one being in all the universe for whom self-exaltation is the highest virtue and the essence of love.

We creatures may not copy the Creator in this. To the degree that we exalt ourselves for another person to enjoy, we are hateful, not loving, because we distract them from the one being who really can satisfy their souls. Therefore, we may not imitate God in his God-ness. God is the one and only absolutely unique being in all the universe for whom self-exaltation is the essence and the foundation of love. It has to be this way if he is God.

We might want him to love like humans love, by making others central, but he can't do that and still be God. He is infinitely valuable in himself. There is none besides God. Therefore, to put it bluntly, he is "stuck" with being magnificent and glorious and all-sufficient and self-sufficient, without any need of us whatsoever. This is the foundation of grace. If you try to make yourself the center of grace, it ceases to be grace. God-centered grace is biblical grace.

My delight is not in God making me the center of the universe. My delight is in God being the center of the universe, forever, and drawing me up into his fellowship, to see him, know him, enjoy him, treasure him, be satisfied in him, for all the days of eternity.

**The Implications of God's God-Centeredness for Mankind**

Now we turn to Part Two. If what I have said so far is true, if it is biblical, then there is a stunning implication for your life. It is this: what you should do is make it your vocation to be as happy as you possibly can be in God. So my call to you in the rest of this chapter, in the name of God Almighty, is that you might make it your eternal vocation to pursue your pleasure with all the might that God mightily inspires within you.

My problem in life, and your problem in life, is not that we are pursuing our pleasure when we ought to be doing our duty. That is not God's or the Bible's assessment of our problem. Lewis had it exactly right in his life-changing sermon, "The Weight of Glory," when he said that our problem is that we are far too easily pleased, not that we are pursuing our pleasure too eagerly. He says that we are like children fooling around making mud pies in the slums because we cannot imagine what a vacation at the beach is like. Our problem is that we are clutching tin idols to ourselves when golden reality stands before us. We are far too easily pleased. The problem with the world is not hedonism; it's the failure of hedonism to go for what is truly satisfying.

And the implication is that you should get up in the morning and say, like George Mueller, say, before you go out and do anything, "I must have my heart happy in God or I will be of no use to anybody. I'll use them and try to get them to satisfy my cravings and my vacancies." If you want to be a person of love, if you want to be released to lay down your life for other people, you must make it your aim to be happy in God.

But we are far too easily pleased. We have settled for such small, short-lived, inadequate, non-satisfying pleasures that our capacities for joy have so shriveled up to the point that we have made joyless duty the essence of virtue so as to conceal our untransformed hearts that cannot be moved by God. How escapist is that? So I am on a campaign in this chapter against the Stoics and Immanuel Kant, the philosopher of the Enlightenment who said that to the degree that you seek your benefit in any moral act, you diminish its virtue. That idea is not in the Bible. It destroys worship, virtue, courage, and God-centeredness everywhere. It elevates man, the virtuous one who does his duty without any view to God to satisfy his soul. Fie on it! May it be gone from our hearts forever!

I'm on a campaign against the sentiment that hangs in the evangelical air. I started on this campaign about 25 years ago, and I've been on it ever since, trying to raise my family in it, build a church on it, write books about it, trying to live it. Little by little the objections come. That's the way you grow. Several of you have said to me that you feel like your world is being turned by this conference. Paradigms are being shaken. Copernican revolutions are in the offing, and that's just the way you start changing. It may take 15 years and objection after objection.

In 1968, I started seeing some of these things with the help of one of my seminary professor, and then C. S. Lewis, and then Jonathan Edwards, and King David, and Saint Paul, and Jesus Christ. And the way that my mind works is that one objection after the other comes up and I cringe, and then I go to the Bible and I weep and cry and struggle and ask and pray and talk. Then little by little the objections refine the vision.

So here are five objections to what I've been saying.

### Five Objections to Answer

1. Does the Bible really teach that you should pursue your joy

with all your heart and mind and soul and strength, or is that just John Piper's clever way of getting attention?

2. What about self-denial? Didn't Jesus say, "If anyone would come after me, let him deny himself?"
3. Doesn't this put too much emphasis on emotion? Isn't Christianity essentially a matter of the will, whereby we make commitments and decisions?
4. What becomes of the noble concept of serving God as a duty when it's hard and you don't feel like it?
5. Doesn't this just put me—and not God—at the center of things?

**1. Does the Bible really teach that you should pursue your joy?**

My answer is yes, and it does so in at least four ways.

### *a) With commandments*

Consider Psalm 37:4: "Delight yourself in the Lord." This is not a suggestion. This is a commandment. If you believe, "Thou shalt not commit adultery" is something you should obey, then you should also obey, "Delight yourself in the Lord."

Or Psalm 32:11: "Be glad in the Lord, and rejoice, O righteous ones, and shout for joy all you upright in heart." Or Psalm 100: "Serve the Lord with gladness."

That's a commandment: "Serve the Lord with gladness!" To the degree that you are indifferent to whether you serve the Lord with gladness or not, you are indifferent to God. He told you to serve him with gladness. Or Philippians 4:4: "Rejoice in the Lord, and again I say, rejoice."

These commands to pursue joy are all over the Bible. We're talking commandments. That's the first way the Bible teaches this.

### *b) With threats*

Jeremy Taylor once said, "God threatens terrible things if we will not be happy." I thought it was clever when I first heard it. But it's not just clever. It's a quotation from Deuteronomy 28:47, and it's devastating. "Because you did not serve the Lord your God with joyfulness and gladness of heart, therefore you shall serve your enemies whom the Lord will send against you." God threatens terrible things if we will not be happy in him. Is that not a warrant for hedonism? Is that not a warrant to making it your life vocation to pursue your joy in God with all your might?

### *c) By presenting saving faith as essentially being satisfied with all that God is for you in Jesus*

For example, Hebrews 11:6: "Without faith it is impossible to please God, for he who would draw near to God must believe that he is and that he is a rewarder of those who seek him." If you would please God, you must have faith. What is faith? Coming to God precisely with the deep conviction that he is going to reward us for coming. If we don't believe that, or if we go to God for any other reason, we do not please God.

Or take John 6:35. Jesus says, "I am the bread of life. He who comes to me will never hunger, and he who believes in me will never thirst." The one who believes in Jesus will never thirst. What does that mean about faith? What is faith? Faith, in the apostle John's theology, is a coming to Jesus for the satisfaction of our souls such that nothing else can satisfy. That's faith. This is simply basic Christianity in language with which many of us are less familiar.

### *d) By defining sin as the insanity of forsaking the pursuit of your pleasure in God*

Sin is the insanity of forsaking the pursuit of your pleasure in God. Jeremiah 2:12–13: "Be appalled, O heavens, be shocked. Be utterly desolate, says the Lord. For my people have committed two great evils. They have forsaken me, the fountain of living waters and have hewed out for themselves cisterns, broken cisterns that can hold no water."

Tell me, what is evil? What is the definition of evil, that which appalls the universe, that causes the angels of God to say, "No! It can't be!" According to Jeremiah 2:12–13, evil is looking at God, the fountain of all-satisfying, living water, and saying, "No, thank you," and turning to the television, sex, parties, booze, money, prestige, a house in the suburbs, a vacation, a new computer program, and saying, "Yes!" That's evil.

In those four ways, at least, the Bible confirms that what I'm saying here is true when I say *devote your life to the pursuit of your satisfaction in God*. So objection number 1 falls.

**2. What about self-denial?**

Didn't Jesus say in Mark 8:35, "Whoever would come after me let him deny himself and take up his cross"? The cross is a place where you die. It's a place of execution. It's not a cranky mother-in-law, or a bad roommate, or a disease in your bones. It's death of the self. So then, am I heretical in calling you to pursue the satisfaction of your souls as a life-vocation? I've felt that objection—and then I read the rest of the verse: "for he who would save his life will lose it, and he who loses his life for my sake will save it." What is Jesus's logic in these verses? The logic is this . . .

> "O my disciples, don't lose your life. Don't lose your life. Save your life! Save your life!"

"How Jesus?"

"Lose it."

"I don't get it. I don't get it Jesus."

"What I mean is—my disciples, my loved ones—lose your life in the sense that you lose everything but me. 'Unless a grain of wheat falls to the ground and dies, it remains alone. But if it dies it bears much fruit.' Die to the world. Die to prestige, die to wealth, die to illicit sex, die to cheating to get ahead, die to the need for people to approve you. Die, and have me."

I believe in self-denial. Deny yourself tin to have gold. Deny yourself sand to stand on a rock. Deny yourself brackish water to have wine. There is no ultimate self-denial—nor did Jesus ever mean it that way.

I believe in self-denial. I believe this word about Jesus from Jesus in Matthew 13:44. "The kingdom of heaven is like a man who found a treasure hidden in a field and, *in his joy*, he went and sold everything he had to buy that field." You call that self-denial? Yes! He sold everything. He counted everything as refuse and rubbish that he might gain Christ.

So, yes, it's self-denial—and no, it isn't ultimate self-denial. There is a self that should be crucified—the self that loves the world. But the new self—the self that loves Christ above all things and finds its satisfaction in him—don't kill that self. That's the new creation. Glut that self on God.

O, I believe in self-denial. I believe in the self-denial that the rich young ruler couldn't understand but that Jesus taught in that moment: "Go sell everything you've got young man and come follow me, and you'll have treasure in heaven." And he wouldn't do it. And Jesus said to his disciples, "It is really hard for a rich man to get into the kingdom of heaven. It's easier for a camel to go through the eye of a needle than for rich people to get into the kingdom of heaven." Then the disciples were absolutely stunned, and they said, "Who then can be saved." And Jesus said, "With men it is impossible. Nobody can have the heart I'm calling for on their own. But with God," he says, "all things are possible." And then Peter pipes up, "We left everything to follow you. What about us? We really sacrificed." And Jesus responds (I wish I knew the tone of his voice) and says, "Peter, no one has left houses or mother or father or brothers or sisters or lands or children for my sake who will not receive back one-hundred fold of mothers, sisters, brothers, lands, and children, in this life—along with persecutions—and in the age to come, eternal life. You cannot sacrifice anything that will not be repaid to you a thousand-fold. Don't pity yourself when your head gets chopped off for me" (see Mark 10:17–31).

Yes, I believe in self-denial. I believe in denying myself everything that would stand in the way of me being satisfied fully in God, and that's how I understand what the Bible means by self-denial. I believe that the great missionaries David Livingstone and Hudson Taylor, having come to the end of their lives and having lost wives and health and everything else except one thing, were absolutely right to say to Cambridge University students and people elsewhere, "I never made a sacrifice." I know what they mean, and you know what they mean. And I believe that Jim Elliot who laid down his life as a young man was absolutely right to say, "He is no fool who gives what he cannot keep to gain what he cannot lose." That's what I believe about self-denial. So objection number 2 falls.

**3. Aren't you making too much out of emotions?**

Isn't Christianity essentially decision? Commitment of the

will? Aren't emotions just tag-along, optional, icing on the cake? You may think that this way of talking about Christianity elevates emotions to an unbiblical place of prominence.

But then we read the Bible—it helps to read the Bible when you're in an argument—and I we see that:

- We are commanded to feel joy: Philippians 4:4, "Rejoice in the Lord."
- We are commanded to feel hope: Psalm 42:5, "Hope in God."
- We are commanded to feel fear: Luke 12:5, "Fear him who can cast both soul and body into hell."
- We are commanded to feel peace: "Let the peace of Christ rule in your hearts" (Colossians 3:15).
- We are commanded to feel zeal: Romans 12:11, "Be aglow (literally 'boil') in the Spirit, never flag in zeal." This is not optional, this is not icing. It's a commandment! "Never flag in zeal."
- We are commanded to feel grief: Romans 12:15, "Weep with those who weep." You don't have an option. You've got to weep, you've got to feel weeping with those who weep.
- We are commanded to feel desire: 1 Peter 2:2, "Earnestly desire the sincere spiritual milk of the word." It's not an option. You can't say, "Well, I can't turn desire on enough, so how can I obey this? It can't really be a command." Wrong! Yes, you cannot turn these feelings on and off at will. No, they are still obligations. Therein lies our desperate condition that we heard about in Part One.

Everything the Bible commands us to do in these passages above, we cannot do simply by willpower or decision or commitment. You can only do it by miracle. Aren't you desperate? Isn't it a desperate thing to be told by Almighty God that you must do what you cannot do? If our hearts were right, we would do them. But we are depraved, and we are commanded to feel tender-heartedness: "Be kind to one another, tender-hearted." We can't just say that forgiveness means saying, "I'm sorry." We must feel it.

We're commanded to feel gratitude. Take a child on Christmas morning who gets a present from grandma—and it's black socks! Yuck! And then his father says to him, "Say thank you to your grandmother." And then the kid says, "Thank you for the socks." That's not what the Bible is talking about. The kid can do that by willpower. But he cannot feel gratitude for those socks by willpower. Neither can you feel gratitude to God by your willpower in accordance with the command in Ephesians 5:20 to "be thankful for everything." Well then, we're done for, unless Almighty God works.

So you can see, I don't buy objection number 3. I don't believe that I'm elevating affections and feelings and emotions higher than the Bible does. I think I'm reinstating them to the place from where a decisionistic, commitment-laden, willpower American we-can-do-it religion dropped them because they're out of our control.

**4. What about the noble vision of serving God?**

Isn't it a duty to serve God? Someone may say, "It doesn't sound like service in your way of talking about Christianity, Piper." It just doesn't sound the same as service—dutiful, rising to the challenge of performing the will of God when it's hard.

To which I have learned now to respond, "Let's look at a few texts that shape the metaphor of servanthood." All metaphors about your relationship to God, whether it's as a servant, or son or daughter, or friend, have elements in them which, if you stressed them, would be false. They also have elements in them which, if you stressed them, would be true. Now what is false and what is true in the analogy of servanthood?

The texts that help us separate the two so that we don't blaspheme when we serve are texts like Acts 17:25: "God is not served by human hands, as though he needed anything. But he himself gives to all men life and breath and everything." *God is not served.* Be careful. He is not served as though he needed you or your service. He doesn't.

Or take a text like Mark 10:45: "The Son of Man came not to be served but to give his life as a ransom for many." *He came not to be served.* Watch out! Watch out! If you undertake to serve him, then you cross his purpose! Perplexing though, isn't it? Paul called himself the servant of the Lord in every letter almost. And here in Acts 17:25 and Mark 10:45, it says that God is not served and that the Son of Man came not to be served. There must be a kind of service that is evil and a kind of service that is good. What is the good service?

The good service is 1 Peter 4:11: "Let him who serves serve in the strength that God supplies, that in everything God may get the glory." God is not served by human hands as though he needed anything. We must find a way to worship, type papers, listen to lectures, drive a car, change a diaper, preach a sermon, in such a way that we are always the receiver. Because the giver gets the glory, and the receiver gets the joy. Anytime we cross Acts 17:25—"God is not served by humans hands [as though he were a receiver,] as though he needed anything"—we blaspheme.

Yesterday I gave an illustration to the leadership crew of this conference from Matthew 6:24 about service. "You cannot serve two masters. Either you'll hate the one and love the other. Or either you'll be devoted to one and despise the other. You cannot serve both God and money." So here we're talking service. How do you serve money? You do not serve money by meeting money's needs. You serve money by posturing your life relentlessly, with all of your energy and time and effort, to benefit from money. Your mind spins with how to make the shrewd investment, how to find the best deal, how to invest where it's low so that it'll go high, and you're consumed with how to benefit from money, because money is your source.

If that's true about the way you serve money, how then do you serve God? It's exactly the same. You posture yourself, and you maneuver your life, and you devote energy and effort and time and creativity to positioning yourself under the waterfall of God's continual blessing, so that he remains the source and you remain the empty receiver. You remain the beneficiary, he remains the benefactor. You remain hungry, he remains the bread. You remain thirsty, he remains the water. You don't ever do the blasphemous role-reversal on God.

We must find a way to serve that is in the strength that God supplies. If I am on the receiving end when I am serving, then I put God in the position of a beneficiary. I become his benefactor, and now I am God. And there are many such religions in the world. So objection 4 falls.

**5. Aren't you just making yourself central?**

"You talk about pursuing your joy and your pleasure," someone might say. "You talk about duty as something else than what we've always known, and you say that we must be careful about service. It sounds to me like you're maneuvering and manipulating biblical language just to make yourself central." That would be the most devastating criticism of all, wouldn't it?

Here's my answer: I've been married to my wife Noël since

December 21, 1968. I love her a lot. We've been through a lot together, both really hard times and really good times. We've seen our teenage kids through some incredibly difficult teenage years. I cry most easily when I think about my sons and my little girl. Suppose on December 21 next year I come home with dozens of long-stem red roses behind my back (one for each year) and ring the doorbell. Noël comes to the door, looks sort of puzzled about why I would be ringing my own doorbell, and I pull the roses out and say, "Happy Anniversary, Noël!" And she says, "Johnny, they're beautiful! Why did you?" And I say, "It's my duty."

Wrong answer.

Let's back it up and try it again.

> [Ding-dong]
>
> "Happy Anniversary, Noël!"
>
> "Johnny, they're beautiful! Why did you?"
>
> "Nothing makes me happier than to buy you roses. In fact, why don't you go change clothes, and we'll go do something special tonight, because there is nothing I would rather do tonight than spend the evening with you."

Right answer.

Why? Why wouldn't she say, "You're the most selfish Christian Hedonist I've ever met! All you ever think about is what makes *you* happy!"

What's going on here? Why is duty the wrong answer and delight the right answer?

If you get this, then you've got what I've been getting at in this chapter. My wife is most glorified in me when I am most satisfied in her. If I try to change our relationship into a service relationship, into a duty relationship, where I do not pursue my pleasure in her, she will be belittled. And so will God.

When you get to heaven and the Father looks at you and says, "Why are you here? Why did you lay down your life for me?" you better not say, "It was my duty to come, because I'm a Christian." You better say, "Where else would I want to go? To whom else could I turn? You are my soul's desire!"

And that is what this Passion conference is about. This conference is about two great things coming together in the 268 Generation from Isaiah 26:8. It is the passion of God for his name and renown, and the passion of my heart to be satisfied in all of my desires. Those are two unshakable things in the universe. And what I hope you have seen is that they are one, because God and his name and his renown are most glorified in me when I am most satisfied in him.

8

# Divine Interruptions

CHRISTINE CAINE

I want to tell you about how my life was interrupted. Not interrupted in a temporary sense; those kinds of interruptions happen all the time. I want to tell you about a divine interruption—the kind of interruption that makes it impossible to go back to the way things once were. These are transformational interruptions, the kind where God forever changes you and sends you into the world to do what Jesus did.

Jesus prayed, I believe, for the Father to interrupt our lives like this. He specifically asked in John 17:15 that His followers not be taken out of the world, but rather that they be sent into the world. It's in being sent into the world—the *real* world—that we are interrupted by what we find there. But God does not bring interruptions into our lives merely to arouse our sympathies; He does so that we might take up the cause of Jesus in a dramatic and world-changing fashion.

That's what happened to me several years ago. I had learned all about the tragedy of the Holocaust through studying German economic history for several years. But despite all the study I had done, something different happened to me when I set foot in Auschwitz.

This was no textbook at university. This was no movie, no book, no picture—this was the devastating reality. There before me were the gates and the fences. The chambers and the ovens. And then there were the shoes. Thousands of shoes. Shoes of the victims, lined up in what was now a museum. Worse even than the volume of shoes was the size of some of them. These were children's shoes; shoes that might have belonged to my own daughters Catherine and Sophia. And standing there, in that place where people were marked not by names or faces but instead by tattooed numbers, my breath caught in my chest.

It was easy until that point to look at this kind of suffering in a clinical way. Tragic, of course, but somewhat faceless. But being there changed the number of six million people from a statistic to a reality. These were six million who had a face and a name. Six million people who once wore shoes. Through tears, I remember crying out to the Lord saying, "God, where was the church? Why did we not lend our voice to this injustice? Where were your people during this time?"

Yes, I know there was a resistance movement. Yes, I know of Bonhoeffer and others who did not sit idly by. But I also know that there were countless others who did nothing. I remember, upon that realization, saying to God, "If there is ever anything like this in my generation, I will not be silent." I did not realize that just nine months later, God would interrupt my life again, not with the past but with the present.

I found myself speaking at a conference in Greece around the time that a little girl named Madeline went missing in Portugal. Her picture was plastered across the TV, in airports, and in magazines—Interpol was searching for this little girl everywhere. I was, of course, very saddened by the disappearance of a little girl, but I didn't know her. I hadn't met her. My sympathies were aroused, but what could I do? The true interruption came during a mundane moment when I was waiting for my bag at an airport terminal. I saw the posters of Madeline that I had seen before, but then I saw a second poster for another girl that was missing. This child was named Sophia—the same name of my second daughter. It was like seeing the shoes from Auschwitz all over again.

Suddenly these missing children weren't numbers. They weren't posters and they weren't statistics. They were real—someone's daughters. Someone's sisters and classmates. I stopped and began to wonder if that was my Sophia on that poster, *what wouldn't I do to find her? What wouldn't I give up to see her safe?* The closest I've ever come to a situation like that was when we lost Sophia once in London for about five minutes; but even for that brief time, I ran around screaming like a mad woman. I didn't care who looked or who saw; I would have given everything I had in that moment to rescue that one who was missing.

I later found out that these children were the alleged victims of human trafficking, something that at that time I didn't even know existed. I assumed that the slave trade was abolished with William Wilberforce but I was dead wrong. On my watch, in my generation, the current state of slavery has been flourishing in the dark rooms of the world. With all our great Christian gatherings, our tremendous churches, our wealth of worship songs and resources, right now in the 21st century, there are more slaves on earth than ever before. It was incomprehensible to me.

How could this be true? How could this happen in our day?

How could the gospel have spread and flourished in so many areas and yet not made a massive dent in something as simple and insidious as slavery? Yet it's true. During our day, more people are being trafficked and sold for labor or sex than ever before in human history.

This is unacceptable not merely from the standpoint of human rights; it's unacceptable from the standpoint of the teaching of Jesus. We could point to any number of Scriptures that tell us this, but the one that continues to interrupt me is found in Luke 10, beginning in verse 30:

> Then Jesus answering said, "A certain man went down from Jerusalem to Jericho, and fell among thieves, who stripped him of his things, wounded him, and departed, leaving him half dead. Now by chance, a certain priest came down that road: and when he saw him, he passed by on the other side. Likewise a Levite, when he arrived at the place, came and looked, and passed by on the other side; but a certain Samaritan, as he journeyed, came where he was: and when he saw him, he had compassion, so he went to him, and bandaged his wounds . . ."

The text goes on, but the key phrase for me continues to be how Jesus described the Samaritan. He "had compassion" on the one who was in great need.

We might be tempted to equate compassion with getting sad watching a movie or hearing a story. That's not compassion; that's sentiment. Compassion isn't compassion until you are actually interrupted. It's not real until it inspires action. It was the action not the sentiment that separated the Samaritan from the others.

The Levite and the priest might well have been very nice people.

Religious even. Perhaps they were even that day hurrying to one or another of their religious activities. I had the sudden realization that though I've always thought of myself as a Samaritan, my inaction revealed me to be much more like the two other figures who passed by. They were so busy going to their next religious service that they walked past the very people God sent them into the world to reach.

Sound familiar? It certainly does to me. For the priest and Levite, and for many of us, people like this man in the ditch are distractions to the ministry. But to God, they are not the distraction; they are the object. That being the case, here's the poignant question for all of us: *What are you going to do, Christine? Are you going to walk past on the other side, hurrying to your next event, or are you going to cross the street and actually get involved?* This was my moment to decide if these people, scattered throughout the world, were going to be people with names and faces or if they were going to turn into just another pair of empty shoes.

With knowledge comes responsibility. We know the slave trade is alive and well right now. We know this, and because we do, we are responsible to do something about it. In our choice about whether to cross the road, we must begin by realizing that at one point or another, we were the one lying in the ditch and Jesus crossed the road for us.

I am a rescued person. I did not discover that I was adopted until I was thirty-three years old. Though our parents never told us the truth, on a single day we discovered this family secret and the truth was jarring to say the least. Suddenly I didn't know who I was anymore. I didn't know whether I was conceived in an adulterous affair or a one-night stand. I didn't know if I was the result of a rape or an underage pregnancy.

As the panic started to set in though, the Lord reminded me

that I didn't have to know those specific facts to know who I am. Because I encountered Jesus, I know something larger and more important than those circumstantial details. The Word of God tells me that I am not the result of a rape or the product of an affair. The Word tells me I am the workmanship of God, reborn in Christ Jesus, specifically for the good work He has prepared for me beforehand to walk in (Ephesians 2:8–10). I may not know who I was, but I know who I am; I have been rescued by the grace of God in Jesus Christ. Jesus crossed the road between heaven and earth so that I might cross the road for the sake of others. I was saved by grace that I might walk in the way Jesus did in the world. This is the plan of God—to use rescued people to rescue people.

When I first began to cross the road, there were a lot of "buts." There always seemed a reason to pause and say, "But God, what about . . ."

*What about my career?*

*What about my reputation?*

*What can I really do?*

Here is another "but" for you to consider, though. One person can do a minimal amount, *but what can an entire generation do?* What can hundreds of thousands of people do when they commit themselves to crossing the road? What might be accomplished if our lives were interrupted so that we become advocates for human rights? What if we committed to use what gifts and talents we've been given for the sake of making a difference in the very world that Jesus sent us into? What might happen if an army of Jesus-following students, teachers, doctors, lawyers, business people, moms, and dads suddenly took hold of our responsibility? Jesus has set us free so that we might set others free. He rescued us so that we might rise up, reach back, and rescue others.

Never before has there been a more important time for us as the rescued people of God to arise. Never before has there been a greater moment for us to take hold of the good works God has prepared for us even before He saved us by His grace. It must be now, for there are people all over the world that have that same destiny prepared before them, and yet are being robbed of it. The truth is the line between the rescued and those who need rescuing is very, very fine.

If I was not born in Australia and instead been born in Greece, Moldova, Romania, Bulgaria, Cambodia, Nepal, or any one of countless other countries, I could have been one of those girls. In fact, if you could see my birth certificate right now, all you would see is a number. I was Number 2508 of 1966. That's it.

It's just another number, just another statistic. It could be anyone of the twenty-seven million slaves in the world right now. But that twenty-seven million must cease to be a number. Just like you and me, these people are living, breathing human beings created in the image of Almighty God, full of God-given destiny and God-given promise. The same Jesus who set me free can set them free, but how will they hear those words if we do not go? How will they ever know the truth if we, together, don't raise our voices and declare that we will not allow this injustice to prevail? The Apostle Paul said that it is for freedom that Christ has set us free, and we must take that declaration to the world.

Not long ago I was sitting at one of our shelters with Sonia, one of fourteen rescued victims. One of these young women, one that wasn't a statistic anymore began telling me about how she was shipped to Istanbul in a container with sixty other girls. During the trip, the oxygen tank broke, and when the crate was actually opened, thirty of the sixty girls were dead.

The ones left alive had no passports because the traffickers had taken them. They were locked in an apartment and then raped several times a day by men wearing law-enforcement uniforms so the girls would not trust the police. Then they were put in a little rubber dingy to be taken from Istanbul to Athens through the Greek islands.

While en route, the traffickers were spotted by a coast guard patrol, and so they threw the girls overboard. Keep in mind these girls were from villages and had barely seen running water, let alone been in a body of water to swim. Only five survived.

Sonia was one of them. She was eventually brought to our shelter when the police raided a brothel in Athens. It was about that time in this unbelievable story that a Russian girl sitting near us, who had been rescued only a day before Sonia, began to yell at me in broken Greek, "Why did you come?"

As best I could, I began to tell her about how Jesus had rescued me and so I wanted to help her. I told her that God has a plan, a purpose, and a destiny for her life; that it didn't matter what she had gone through, God was big enough to redeem her past.

But it's what she said to me next that I'll never forget. As I was telling her this good news, she yelled back at me, "If what you are telling me about your God is true, then why didn't you come sooner?"

*Why hadn't I come sooner?*

Those are haunting words. What is so important in our temporal lives that will distract us from the eternal purpose God put us on the earth for? What deserves more attention than the very people Jesus died for? Safety, comfort, and security are not the goal of Christianity; freedom is. Because it is, we must rise together to declare that this will not happen on our watch. Not today. Not ever again.

There's just one more story I want to share with you, this one specifically about my five-year-old, Sophia. She loves flashlights, so I bought her one at the store. Standing there, in the checkout line, she was frustrated because she could not see the light. Her light was ineffective in all the light already in that massive room. So Sophia, in the way only a five-year-old can, yelled out to me, "Mummy, can we please go and find some darkness?" She understands that light works most effectively in one place—where there's darkness. That darkness is not to be feared when you have the light.

We don't need to fear the darkness of the world. We don't need to fear the statistics. We don't need to fear the injustice or the traffickers. We do not because we have the light. Because we do, we must be asking the same question that my little girl was: "Can we please go find some darkness?"

*For more from Christine Caine go to christinecaine.com*

# 9

# Passion, Purpose, and Designer Jeans

LOUIE GIGLIO

If you've ever been to a Passion Conference, you know something incredibly powerful happens when you put tens of thousands of people in the same arena, at the same time, united around the same cause. It creates a special atmosphere, and the result can be an unusual synergy of purpose and clarity as we, the Body of Christ, see more clearly what life is all about. Together, we understand more accurately where we fit into God's great, global plan. The question is, what happens next? And this is where I feel we have some refining and reframing to do.

Often, I hear:

"I'm moving to East Asia."

"I'm headed to the Middle East."

"I'm joining this organization or pursuing that avenue of ministry."

"I'm giving my summer away for the sake of the gospel."

"I want to plant a church."

As you would imagine, responses like this follow every Passion event. A young man or woman catches a vision of the greatness of Jesus and knows whatever He is a part of is going to last forever. They know much of the world has yet to hear about Him, and they want to do their part to spread His fame. But are these kinds of responses the only way you can share in that mission?

Don't get me wrong, obviously those things are great things. In fact, they are big things! But in some ways, they might also be easier things. I know, that sounds like I have it backwards, doesn't it? You think the harder decision is to leave home and share the gospel in a foreign land. It's harder to give up a summer to serve people you've never met in a faraway place than to stay close by home in a summer job. But the truth is sometimes it's easier to get really excited about a one-time opportunity than it is to be amped about the day-to-day life that awaits a normal guy or girl right where they are.

So let me be clear: our goal at Passion isn't just to get as many of you as possible to go around the world to places where Jesus hasn't been worshipped fully. Our goal is broader than that. We are definitely *for* a global mind-set, but the globe also includes the people who live next door. So, what we're after is something more long lasting than an initial push out the door. We're after a spark for Jesus inside you that might push you across the world, but will no doubt push you across the hallway in your dorm or across the cubical in your office. We are after an awakening of purpose that will lead you to a lifestyle that says *I want you to know that I care about you, and I want to live a life that shows you over the course of time that there is something real and powerful about the risen Son of God.*

So no, I'm not necessarily trying to get you to Africa today, though hopefully you'll get there at some point. We are, however, trying to get you back to your hometown and that regular routine you're going to face day after day. I want you to be open to living among the nations, but excited about your home turf, *your Jerusalem*. I want God to send you back to your everyday world fully awake to the greatness of Jesus.

For some of you that *will* mean you sense God's unmistakable calling on your life toward full-time ministry. Fantastic! I'd be honored to know you walked out the doors of Passion with a God-birthed desire to be a church planter, a preacher, a Bible teacher, or a worship leader. You might be thinking right now about giving your life to an unreached people in a remote part of the world or a city that hasn't been penetrated with the name of Jesus. We couldn't be more supportive of that direction. On the other hand, God's pathway for you might look different. Like, for example, blue jeans.

*Blue jeans?*

Yes, blue jeans!

Think about it. You've got a pair. I have a pair—several, actually. And because we have them, somebody has to make them. And somebody has to sell them. And, it's quite possible that in an arena this size there's someone sitting here right now thinking, *That's me*. You're the one that is thinking about a fashion-forward designer jean. You think about jeans more than the rest of us combined. You dream about jeans. Every now and then, you turn to a blank page in your journal and sketch jeans. You're into fabrics, and you like to feel the different kinds of cotton brush. You check out the different washes. You examine the stitching on the pockets. In fact, you've already got an idea for a microbusiness brewing in your head. You can see your first store in your mind, and you can envision how your brand is going to start to spread. You can see other larger stores carrying your line. You love jeans. And maybe you even feel a little uncomfortable about it in an environment like this, maybe even a little guilty.

Aren't we trying to win the world to Jesus here? And you're thinking about fashion? Seriously? We have a worldwide mission to go make disciples. It's a movement initiated by the Son of God—and you're thinking about blue jeans? If that's you, then you may be wondering if something's wrong with you. Everyone else is talking about ministry, and you're dreaming about owning your own clothing store. Maybe you feel left out of the reach-the-world equation. But I've got some good news for you. It's freeing news, because those jeans in your dreams might just be the means through which God has planned for you to bring His grace to the world. That's what the Apostle Paul seems to be getting at when he writes:

> And whatever you do, whether in word or deed, do it all in the name of the Lord Jesus, giving thanks to God the Father through him. (Colossians 3:17)

Those first four words are words of freedom: *and whatever you do. Whatever* is an encompassing word, and in case you didn't get the first four words, Paul amplifies them by adding "in word or deed." That, my friends, is fairly comprehensive, speaking to the fact that you can walk a lot of different roads as long as you are moving with the central purpose that motivates us all.

I wish so badly I had heard this truth when I was entering my twenties. Unintentionally on the part of those I learned from, I grew up with the idea that some vocations mattered more to God than others. Yet, what God is breathing through the hand of Paul as he writes frees us to embrace the unique passions that fuel our hearts. Why does this matter? Each of us is wired with different abilities, leanings, inclinations, and aptitudes. You might be wired for architecture, business leadership, innovation, education, filmmaking, the arts, engineering, or any number of other things. You've got crazy dreams inside you, but maybe like me you're not sure if some of the vision and passion that keeps you up at night fits in the Church, or in God's plan.

But the great news is that Paul seems to be legitimizing all of the stuff inside you, affirming that your particular passion can be leveraged for the sake of the kingdom of God. Now, Paul's words do eliminate some options from our lives, because there are a lot of things we can't do in the name of Jesus. But that's not the point of this passage. God isn't asking you to focus on what you can't do (you can't sin to the glory of God), but encouraging you in whatever you can do! When reading Paul's words, you discover that the division you might be trying to navigate—this "so-called" line in the sand between what is spiritual and what is secular—really doesn't exist. And when you embrace this, any line of thinking that tells you God can only use you through a "preapproved" spiritual vocation begins to fade away. You begin to see that you can glorify God in many different ways, not only by getting a theological degree or by picking up a guitar to become a worship leader. I say this as someone who *does* have a theological education and *has* led worship for a season in life. So, obviously, I am humbled and thrilled with God's calling on my life. Yet, I have come to embrace what A. W. Tozer says when he writes, "It's not what a man does that determines whether his (or her) work is sacred or secular, it's why he does it. The motive is everything." It is not your passion that determines whether or not your life honors God and is useful to others, it's your purpose. Why are you doing what you do?

The category of options is wide open to you. Whatever you do, whatever building you build, whatever stocks you trade, whatever jeans you design, know that you are sons and daughters of God, united under the mission to bring glory to God in whatever venue you find yourself. Paul doesn't say you should deny the dreams inside you; he says to elevate them for a higher purpose. In fact, he says to embrace them with everything you've got. "Do it all," he says. Whatever it is you do, don't do it halfheartedly. Whether you're a pastor, an artist, a lawyer, a landscaper, or a NASCAR pit-crew member, do it with everything you've got. Live in such a way that, in word and deed, all the gifts, all the vision, all the passion, and everything God has put inside you is used to the fullest possible extent. Bring it all, and bring it hard. Just do it with and for the right purpose.

And your purpose is this—do it all in the name of the Lord Jesus, giving thanks to God the Father through Him. That's the transcendent purpose for the building you're going to build, the lesson you're going to teach, the professional journal you're getting published in, the magazine you will write for, the repair service you will operate, the family you will raise. And that's the eternal value in those jeans you're going to design. So work as hard as you can to do it as best you can, and remember why you're doing it in the first place.

Remembering the *why* keeps you from losing your balance as you walk the tightrope of loving Jesus and doing something meaningful in a world that often rejects Him. And remembering what truly lasts (His name) helps you stay in touch with the fact that no matter how awesome that building is, no matter how revolutionary your theory is, no matter how hip your jeans are, eventually your building is coming down, your theory will be eclipsed, and your jeans will go out of style. When you are embracing that, you are remembering that the whole story of the universe is moving to a God-determined conclusion, one in which this broken earth is going to be destroyed as God makes all things new.

That's key, because knowing how and where the story ends helps you avoid one of the huge dangers inherent in living out the "whatever" that's inside you—namely falling in love with what you create and losing your love for the One who created you. You could read Colossians 3:17 and suddenly feel divine permission to run after that passion in your heart. That's good, and that's right. But while you're doing the "whatever, in word or deed" that you're wired to do, you must remember your passion has a greater purpose, and the purpose is going to outlive the passion. If you get this part straight, you're on the right track. So the question, then, is how do you do your "whatever" in the name of the Lord Jesus Christ, giving thanks to the Father through Him?

I suppose you could think that as you are making these jeans, you include a little hidden nod to Jesus in every pair. Maybe there's a tag on the back that if you're looking in a mirror the reverse of it says "John 3:16." Or maybe there's a little fish on the pocket on the front. Or maybe you pray over the thread before you put it in the seam. Yeah, maybe you could print a tiny Bible verse on the back of a little label inside every pair of jeans.

Or maybe it's simpler than that. Maybe you don't need a fish sign on every single thing you do to tell the world you are living for a greater cause. Maybe the fish symbol is replaced with you, living a different kind of life. You become a symbol of something different to the world.

For starters, people see your purpose in your end product. The way you make jeans in the name of Jesus is to make it your aim to produce *the best jeans that can possibly be made*. You don't make halfhearted jeans, rather, you make a brand of jeans that not only can survive in the cutthroat fashion environment, you make jeans that will win a share of the marketplace. So with that in mind, you go to fashion school, and you work hard. You bust it to get the right internship, and you work harder than everyone else and absorb everything you can. You show up first and leave last. Yet every day you walk in God's favor as a loved and accepted son or daughter.

You are humble, not proud. You are learning, not teaching. You take every opportunity to get trained, to hone your skill, to develop your passion, to get more experience. Why? Because you have a divine gift wired into your makeup, and you want to do the very, very, very, very, very, very best you can when you make your jeans. You pay the price, and you don't give up when times are hard or opposition comes. You quietly walk with God, even when you can't publically preach about Him in a meeting. Yet, you operate with a massive advantage: you are working from acceptance and not *for* it. You strive to be the best, not so that you can be applauded by someone else, but *because* you are already dearly loved by God.

Then, when you are ready to start making the jeans, what sets you apart? You run a fair business, you treat your employees well, and you do everything you do in a way as to reflect the very life of Jesus. You don't have to tell everyone you're doing it for Jesus. If you do it well, eventually they will ask you what sets you apart.

But let's not stop there. Let's just assume that you make something happen in the jeans world. You get a little business going. It starts out in your garage, but all of a sudden it turns into an enterprise. People are loving your jeans, and the business shifts into high gear. Clothing reps are contacting you, you get floor space in the right stores, and the media picks up on your product. All of a sudden the world is at your door. Wow! That's what the mission is all about at Passion, right? The purpose is to go to the whole world and tell them about Jesus. Yet, because of your conviction and sacrifice to be the very best, the world comes to you. And, in that moment, your passion turned—product becomes your platform to share your faith with those who want to know how you did it.

But let's not stop there. The jeans are flying off the shelves now, and all of a sudden you're putting cash in the bank. Now what are you going to do with that cash? That's when you remember the difference between your passion and your purpose. And you decide that you don't need all that money, so you say, "With the money that we make from our designer jeans, part of it instantly goes to an unreached people group somewhere in the world." What if your organization went there a couple of times a year to serve in that area? And then what if you started recruiting more and more people to serve there? Then there's an orphanage that's started. Then wells are dug. Then business investments are launched in that area. Churches are planted, and suddenly you've got a movement for good on your hands. All because of those jeans. All because of your "whatever."

That's when you know your purpose is greater than your passion; it's when your passion becomes the means to your purpose. Are you starting to see it? We have to infiltrate culture before we can influence culture. And we infiltrate culture by doing the "whatever" that has been woven into our hearts in the name of Jesus. In the end, it's not about what you do; it's about doing whatever you do for the sake of reflecting the greatness of the Son of God to the world.

Here's how Paul puts it in 2 Corinthians 4:6:

> For God, who said, "Let light shine out of darkness," made his light shine in our hearts to give us the light of the knowledge of God's glory displayed in the face of Christ.

In other words, this same God who spoke existence to the universe also shined His love and His light into our hearts and gave us His light in the face of Jesus Christ. We now have the knowledge of the glory of God in the face of Christ. But Paul goes on. He tells us in verse seven that "we have this treasure in jars of clay to show that this all-surpassing power is from God and not from us." We are carriers of this treasure—the knowledge of the glory of God in the face of Christ—in ordinary containers. Pots of clay. And we carry it in these ordinary containers to show how great the God is who planted the treasure there to begin with.

Again, the temptation is going to be for your passion to replace your purpose. For you to start thinking it's about the jeans and not about the Jesus behind them. When that happens, when the passion becomes the purpose, the waters get so muddy that nobody ever hears the story behind the passion. The glory, the money, the fame, the recognition—those things are going to come for some of you. But there are some key things that we must remember to help us stay straight and remember the difference between the passion and the purpose. I think we can sum these things up in three phrases.

The first phrase is this: love God supremely. As a believer, you have the light of Christ within you, but that light stays burning only as you continue to be in fellowship with Him. When you are in fellowship with Jesus, you remind yourself that even in your passions and desires, Jesus is first and foremost. If you don't, the result is going to be emptiness. You may still be great at what you've been gifted to do, but in the midst of your accomplishments and wealth you will mask a heart that says, "It's not enough." So we set our hearts not on our passions, but on the God behind them. We must love God supremely.

Second, as you love God supremely, you must pursue excellence in what you do. In that excellence you engage the culture around you. For too long, Christians have given excellence over to the rest of the world while we stay inside of our sanitized Christian subdivision where our work doesn't have to stand up to that of the "real world." We've got to take excellence back. We can't settle for less than the best. So you have to link His calling on your life and your newfound purpose to use that calling to make much of His name with a desire to create things in and for the world that reflect His beauty.

In truth, I don't have solid ground to stand on here. As a college student I failed out of college. Twice. I got grades that—before college—I didn't know existed. But hey—I was a youth pastor while I was going to school, right? That made it okay to be miserable in my studies, because I was serving God . . . right?

God didn't think so. Neither did the academic dean at Georgia State University. In fact, I remember a conversation with God that went something like this. I had been "asked" to take some time off by the university and one day was driving to class at the junior college I had enrolled in, which I was also failing at.

> God: "You sense My call on your life, don't you? That's good. I want you to preach My word. I want you to communicate My truth. I want you to use the communication skills and creative gifts I have wired into you to tell people about Jesus. So I need you to get trained. You are going to want to go to grad school eventually, right?"
>
> Me: "Yes."
>
> God: "Well, that's going to require a Bachelor's degree first."

*Hmmm.* Something clicked. My right here and now suddenly was a part of God's forever and unfolding plan. I literally took the next exit off the freeway and headed toward downtown Atlanta.

I drove to Georgia State University, parked, and went up to the dean of my school's office. I had no appointment, so I camped out by his assistant's desk until there was a tiny crack in the schedule and I could speak to him. When I finally did, I decided to go with the truth and not concoct some grand reason for the ill that had befallen me: "I've blown it and I need to get back into school. God has called me to go to seminary, and I need a Bachelor's degree to do that. I really didn't connect the dots before, but there is a purpose on my life, and GSU is a vital part of the plan. Could you please have mercy on me and help me get back in school this term?" I won't bore you with the rest of the conversation, but it was pretty entertaining when he asked for my student ID number and pulled up my transcript on his computer.

Yet, even though the term had already started, I walked out of his office with a course schedule in my hand, and I went to a class the very next day. Something switched inside of me, and I saw what was right before me as the proving ground of my calling. I knew that to get to the place God wanted me (and the place I was dreaming about) I needed to be excellent today. That has to happen to you, too.

But just because you see the plan doesn't mean that every step you take is going to work out. Loving God supremely and pursuing excellence doesn't mean you will automatically be successful. When you choose to engage culture with excellence, there's a chance you are going to fail. That's incredibly frightening, but it's true. But remember, regardless of the results, you are embraced by the Father. You're already marked and held by Him. And the good news is that you can fail and still be loved by God. Facts are facts—your business might not make it. Your job could get downsized. Your boutique may go under. But when that happens, you know what God will say?

"Guess you missed on that one, but let's try another idea. I've still got you in my embrace, and we'll be okay together." So go for it. Take a risk. Reach farther. Don't be afraid to fail. You have more than a safety net beneath you. You have the arms of God around you. Love Him supremely, engage the culture with excellence, and don't be afraid.

The third phrase is this: root and connect your life in a community of faith. Let me take you back to Colossians 3. Verse 15 says, "Let the peace of Christ rule in your hearts, since as members of one body you were called to peace. And be thankful. Let the message of Christ dwell among you richly as you teach and admonish one another with all wisdom through psalms, hymns, and songs from the Spirit, singing to God with gratitude in your hearts."

Did you get that? Pursue your passion, whether it's in entertainment, business, education, or full-time ministry. Go for it, and as you do, stay connected to the community of faith, the local church, so that the people of God can walk with you in this process so that you can be true to what God has called you to do. God has given us the great gift of each other, and our job isn't just to sit together in a worship service; it's to remind each other of what God has put inside us. It's to spur each other on and help us remember the greatness of the purpose that all our passions are wound up inside. And that community, the church, is what keeps us from going off the rails and replacing our purpose with our passion.

So many people start so well. They say, "I'm going to take my place in the public square and make a difference for Jesus." But at the end of the day, they just do the former and not the latter. And in most cases, the common thread is they lose their connection to the church. Often, for good reason, because the church is ill-equipped to launch arrows into the minefield of the world, where nuance and deference are needed as we make good on our calling while maintaining our spiritual integrity.

Going back to what I said at the beginning: sometimes going across the street is harder than going around the world. But our calling is to Jerusalem, Judea, and to the ends of the earth.

Let's say you are called to another country as a missionary. Sure it's a sacrifice and a hard road. But at least everyone knows why you are there and you get the approval, attention, and applause of the church. But let's say you are an investment banker knee deep in derivatives every day, and you are having major influence in the lives of hurting people on the top end of the socioeconomic spectrum. You are leading a firm with skill and courage while using the money you are making to foster generosity around the world and using the platform of your accomplishments to quietly guide people into a relationship with Jesus. Will you get the same applause from your local congregation?

Or let's assume you go to a third-world country to tell strangers about Jesus. That is a hard road to walk, but so is walking it out in front of two suite-mates in your university who are skeptical of faith and clueless of their need for Jesus. So the burden rests on the church to seek to understand and the person to seek to stay engaged. "The righteous will flourish like a palm tree, they will grow like a cedar of Lebanon; planted in the house of the LORD, they will flourish in the courts of our God" (Psalm 92:12–13).

The heartbeat of Passion is to see Jesus lifted high, not just in an event arena, but in the everyday arenas of real life. And that happens not because of a conference, and it's not measured in a four-week mission trip. It happens when God switches a light on inside of you and you begin altering your view of every single environment you find yourself in—day in and day out. It happens when you start living a visible and observable life, one that is alive to the greatness of Jesus. It happens when someone breaks out of the "Christian bubble" and gets the attention of the world. It's then, regardless of where you are on the planet—whether you're in Mozambique or buying a head of lettuce at the grocery store—that you get the chance to share something amazing. You get to share about this God that's at work inside of you.

So let's go together. Let's step into the "whatever." And as we do, let's celebrate the purpose that all of us have in common: "For your name and renown are the desire of our souls."

# 10

# Sowing the Seeds

BETH MOORE

I love unconditional promises. There aren't that many in life when you really think about it. Promises with no strings attached, I mean. Absolute assurances that *this* will always bring *that*. The law of the harvest is one of those promises. Galatians 6:7–9 says, "Do not be deceived: God cannot be mocked. A man reaps what he sows. The one who sows to please his sinful nature, from that nature will reap destruction; the one who sows to please the Spirit, from the Spirit will reap eternal life. Let us not become weary in doing good, for at the proper time we will reap a harvest if we do not give up."

God instituted the law of the harvest at the very beginning of time. From the first whisper of creation, as He set nature in motion and gave it its course. He then confirmed it in Genesis 8:22 after the flood. "As long as the earth endures, seedtime and harvest, cold and heat, summer and winter, day and night will never cease." Seedtime and harvest will never end, and what is true in the ecological realm, God has also ordained to be true in the spiritual realm.

Simply put, present actions have profound future effects. You can count on it. One hundred percent guarantee. If you will sow into the things of the Spirit, you will reap from the Spirit. But what does it mean exactly to sow into a harvest?

God has ordained in His sovereignty that you would have considerable power and influence over your future. You and I both have dirt underneath our fingernails. We are all sowing something. You may not even realize you are throwing anything out into that field, but the seed of a future harvest is hitting the ground as we speak. But what if we became intentional about what we are sowing? Instead of broadcasting seed at random, what if we began to be strategic? Future-oriented, consciously, and systematically thinking about the future effects of our present actions?

God did not create us to be holy victims. We're not scapegoats of the divine will. We are His sons and daughters. He has invited us to partner with Him in what He is doing on this planet, at this hour. We can be a part of His harvest. John 15:8 says, "This is to my Father's glory, that you bear much fruit, showing yourselves to be my disciples." Understand this clearly: it is to your Father's glory that *your life*—not just your pastors, favorite role models, or your worship leader's life, but *yours*—bear fruit that is a part of the massive harvest of God. You are meant to sow strategically into the chronicled history of the kingdom of God.

I am praying that God will raise up history changers in this generation. I'm weary of events. Tired of Bible parties. The kind where we talk about things we will never do. That dark world out there needs fewer people who are interested in rallies and more who are interested in laying their lives down for the sake of Christ and sowing seed that will mean something to somebody. But we will need to be deliberate about the kind of seed we throw down.

At a conference I was leading recently, I asked the audience, women of all ages, what the bottom line is for them. When all was said and done, what did they want their lives to have been about? I gave them a minute or so to think it through. When I was pretty sure most people had considered a response, I asked them another question. "Are you presently on the path that will take you in that very direction?" After a moment's silence, shouts started reverberating from all over the room: "No!"

Exactly what do we think is going to happen? That we'll get to the eleventh hour and then suddenly change courses, hop tracks, get really spiritual, our flesh dying to the passions of this world, and fulfill our God-ordained destiny and make a measurable difference in our final five minutes? It doesn't work like that. I don't mean this with the least hint of condescension, because I would have answered the same question the same way plenty of times, but just because it's common doesn't mean it should continue. When you know the direction you want to go you must sow the seeds that will take you there. So I'll ask you the same question I asked them while I consider it myself: Are you presently on the path that will take you in the direction that leads to an end result you want your life to be about?

Our culture of ever-increasing immediate gratification fights like a tireless iron man against us. Think how few things we're forced to wait for and, when we are, how little patience we have with them. At times, I'll think the second coming of Christ is going to happen before my laptop can restart. The seconds feel like minutes because my discipline to actually wait for something is so wildly diminished. We can instantly see if our text messages were delivered. We can instantly self-publish on a blog. We can DVR a show and skip through the commercials.

But to reap a harvest of the Spirit, we need patience. God brings it about in His own time according to what He has planned. What if He asks your generation to sow the seed, but another generation reaps the harvest?

Would the seed still be worth sowing?

That's the way history is changed: from generation to generation, one doing the sowing, another doing the most bountiful part of the reaping.

There are many specific applications to the law of the harvest, but I want to set just one before you from the parable of the sower. Luke 8:11 says, "The seed is the Word of God." It is impossible to overemphasize the importance of that scripture. We can have a passion to worship God that is profuse and overflowing, but without a passion for God's Word the enemy can devour us. We are sitting ducks, completely vulnerable for seduction, with a pursuit of God that does not include Scripture.

That's my story. As a college student I had a heart to love God and to serve Him. I actively enjoyed talking about Him and telling other people about Him. By my early twenties I knew without a doubt that I would spend my life serving Him, but I had not fortified myself with the Word of God. And the enemy came for me.

Most of us understand that sowing Scripture into our lives is important and worthwhile, but for some reason we just can't get into it. We want to like it, but it never sticks. I understand and I've been there. Think of the Scripture like it's your food for the day. You are going to eat somewhere that day and, in all probability, multiple places: maybe the cafeteria or your apartment, or you're going to drive through and grab something. Now, instead of physical food, think Scripture. Where and at what time of day will you consume the Word of God? For me, I love for it to be as

I'm getting started in the morning. Isaiah 50:4–5 motivate me over and over.

> The Sovereign LORD has given me an instructed tongue,
> to know the word that sustains the weary.
> He wakens me morning by morning,
> wakens my ear to listen like one being taught.
> The Sovereign LORD has opened my ears,
> and I have not been rebellious;
> I have not drawn back.

These verses suggest that we may well have a gifted ability to hear from God in the morning. I love that thought. It even intimates that we might hear something from God that equips us to speak encouragement to someone who is exhausted by life and difficulty. The "someone" is sometimes myself. It also suggests that giving God little opportunity to speak to me is rebellion.

People will often say, "I just don't have time in the morning to get with God in the Bible." It doesn't have to be an hour. We don't have to read three chapters. Sometimes you can absorb more by really thinking through three verses. But you take in your daily bread and you listen.

Remember that God is inviting you into dialogue. He is speaking to you through His Word. So what do you do when someone talks to you? You talk back. For instance, what are you thinking as you're reading? Perhaps it's, *Lord, I'm so sleepy this morning. I can barely keep my eyes open.* Okay, then say it to Him. Maybe you're thinking, *Lord, I don't understand what I just read. I am clueless here.* Say it to Him. Perhaps you are reading along and the subject matter reminds you of someone you know. Say it to Him. Use that word from God as substance for prayer. Maybe you're thinking as you stumble on a passage that it's one of the coolest things you've ever read or wondered where that verse has been for the last ten years. So, say *that* to Him. Engage in dialogue with Him in His Word. Talk back.

Read-respond. Read-respond.

Keep ever before you that the Bible encases the inspired words of God (2 Timothy 3:16). Have respect for it. Ask God to increase your awe toward it. Read it at times as if His Spirit is relaying it straight to your heart, and then speak back to Him what you're thinking. Interact. We're not talking about something weird here, and it's not very likely to send you into a trance. We're talking about a genuine relationship. Think about every authentic one you have. How would you carry on a close relationship without regular conversations? We're talking here about dialoguing with a God who still chooses to speak words of life to those who listen.

When God talks, talk back.

Several years ago, Keith and I were in Angola doing some work in hunger relief. It's something we both are moved by God to do, and we are supercharged by doing it together. Angola spent years in a devastating civil war. The land has been ravaged, decimated, and neglected. To this day, many people are terrified to wander away from main rural roads. Leftover landmines could hide indiscriminately just below the surface. Tens of thousands of Angolans are starving to death. Our job was to help facilitate and serve a bean-based porridge out of big cauldrons to the hundreds waiting in line. The worst part is that the program only has enough support to provide food for the children in the villages where it exists. They receive first access because they have the highest risk for malnutrition. But it is also heartbreaking to see others standing by, hungry.

In our third or fourth village, one of the ministry leaders was describing the cycle of despair the region was stuck repeating. He said, "We gave them seed to plant their own food, but they were so hungry that, instead of planting the seeds, they ate them."

They ate the seeds. Fathom that for a moment.

I was horrified. I couldn't get the irony out of my thoughts for months. Eventually my thoughts drifted back to America, where many of us are stuck in our church culture cul-de-sac. And I was horrified for us too.

I thought about how many times you and I come into contact with the seed of Luke 8:11, the Word of God. We receive it through sermons, podcasts, books, television, personal reading, Twitter, or maybe through a friend's text that day. We could even have portions memorized, but in all of that contact we never end up actually sowing the Word. In other words, we can eat it. Our appetites can get satiated on it, and it can taste amazing. We are spiritually full, but nothing changes. Our lives aren't any different than they were, and no harvest results. Why? Because we ate the seed and did not sow it into the reality of our experience.

God's Word was not meant to build up our theology. It was meant to change our reality. God delivered His Word to us to make us victors, not scholars. I'm all for studying the Scripture, but if all that changes about us is the level of our intellect, we are eating our seed, not sowing it.

Think about how many times you've heard that God has forgiven you. Even if you are new to faith, you've probably heard it at least ten times. For others, the tally could be reaching the hundreds. We hear it in sermons, read it in books, and sing about it in songs. But did we actually sow the seed into our reality? If we have sown that seed of God's complete forgiveness through the cross into our own life's soil, and let it go down deep where transformation takes place, we will weep over it, we'll have to talk about it, and, beloved, we will rejoice over it. It will bring about a true-to-life documentable harvest. Psalm 32:1 says, "Blessed is he whose transgressions are forgiven, whose sins are covered." The word "blessed" in that verse comes from a Hebrew word that means "happy." So, if you and I really sow the forgiveness of God into our lives, we'd be happy about it. That's what the psalmist is saying. It would show up on us. There would be a harvest.

But how in the world do we sow the seed into the reality of our lives instead of just eating it? James 1:21 says, "Therefore, get rid of all moral filth and the evil that is so prevalent and humbly accept the word planted in you, which can save you." The saving James is referring to is more than just receiving eternal life. He's talking about our deliverance. God's Word was meant to work for our real-life temptations. I'm talking about when you are at the peak, feeling overwhelmed, when the enemy's crosshairs are pointed at you, and you're in crisis. You get down on your knees and you plant the Word of God right into the middle of that temptation.

It's important to remember that a harvest takes patience. Sometimes we expect to get up off our knees and be completely fulfilled and fixed, all fleshly craving disintegrated. If we have chosen to plant the seed, not just eat it, then we have to walk by faith. We must continue to believe that in time that seed will—without a single doubt—bring about a harvest.

For example, say you have a brother or sister with whom you need to make amends. So out of obedience to God you humble yourself before that person and say, "I was wrong, and I'm sorry." But, that person won't say it back. We walk away, and instead of feeling victory, we feel really badly or, more likely, we feel annoyed.

At that point we have two choices. The next time we can refuse to humble ourselves, or we can trust that God will do what He says He will do and He will produce a harvest through our obedience.

There are words in Psalm 126 that have come to mean so much to me. It says in verses 5 and 6, "Those who sow in tears will reap with songs of joy. He who goes out weeping, carrying seed to sow, will return with songs of joy, carrying sheaves with him." That is a promise. An absolute biblical guarantee. When you go through a season of extreme difficulty, a time of suffering, if you continue to believe God's Word, even though everything inside of you says to let go, He will bring a harvest of joy. You sow the seed in tears and you will come forth bearing sheaves of gladness. It's a promise. Sometimes the harvest will be all the more amazing and meaningful because you know good and well God watered that seed with your own tears.

That's where the Word has to be, down into the soil of our real lives. It was meant to be practical and not just high and lofty spirituality. We must sow the Spirit into the real, live dust and dirt of our experience on planet Earth.

I mentioned earlier that the enemy came for me in my early twenties. He truly did. I was drawn to the pit with a very strong carnal appetite. I was at war with myself because I really did want to love God. During those days if this very message had come to me, my frame of mind was such that I would've heard the first snippet of Galatians 6:7–9 only. I would have locked into, "Do not be deceived: God cannot be mocked. A man reaps what he sows." And I would have totally missed the idea of sowing to please the Spirit. I would not have heard it because I would have been terrified of what was coming.

The punishment.

The smackdown.

Whatever's coming, I deserve it.

I earned it.

I can do nothing about it.

Is anybody else unable to get past Galatians 6:7 and onto verses 8 and 9? So, what do you do if you know you have been sowing carnality, but you've not yet reaped the harvest of it yet? First, fall on your face and repent. Sometimes fear is the appropriate response. Let that fear drive you facedown, nostrils to the ground, carpet fibers up in your nasal passages. It's a very biblical posture. Second, ask for His mercy. God's mercy is new every single morning. It arrives with the sun. Thank God that according to Psalm 103:10, "He does not treat us as our sins deserve." And use that mercy to obey right now. Don't let past mistakes delay today's obedience. When the power of God's Word comes to you, the power is there to respond in that anointing.

If you're like I was, you desperately need to ask God to put Matthew 15:13 into immediate action. "Every plant that my heavenly Father has not planted will be pulled up by the roots." What is in your life that your heavenly Father did not plant? Don't just keep mowing it down. Let him pull it up by the roots. Maybe you planted some things that shouldn't be there or maybe somebody else threw that seed down. There is a time to plant and a time to uproot. Let him pull it up until it's out, in Jesus' Name.

And if the consequences of past mistakes do come your way, don't fight them. God disciplines His children sometimes. Humble yourself and receive it. What else can you do? You can be arrogant, deny any wrongdoing, and delay the lesson. The better way is to cooperate with God and His favor and approval *will be on you.* In the meantime you start sowing the wheat, the good seed, among those tares as furiously as you know how until you begin to choke out every single one of those weeds.

Start becoming intentional about what you sow into your life and you can change how history will be written for you. And maybe for many others. Sow the things of the Spirit and reap the things of the Spirit. There's no reason not to start today.

A young woman I dearly loved was tragically killed in an automobile accident right before Christmas several years ago. She was the kind of person you wanted to be like. She loved Jesus. Faithfully taught His Word to anyone who would listen. Loved people. Loved to laugh. She'd pursued education in Christian counseling and was one of my favorite people on our ministry team. She had no intention of living a life where God wouldn't be glorified. She was only in her midtwenties and was already truly extraordinary.

As the news was spreading about her passing, a mutual friend called me and filled me in on some of the details of what happened that day. Stephanie was on her way to her hometown to spend the holidays with her mom when an eighteen-wheeler hit ice on the interstate, lost control, crossed the median, and hit her car head-on. One of her passions was Scripture memory, and in her car she had stacks of Scripture cards she'd been processing and memorizing. When the collision occurred those cards were strewn all over the place. So picture it. There at the scene of the accident among the broken glass and twisted metal, was sewn the Word of God hitting the soil of this earth the way it had hit the soil of her heart.

It will mark me forever.

Your life may be totally put together. It may be a total mess or somewhere erratically in between.

No matter. Sow the seed of the Word of God.

And you *will* produce a harvest.

"For a man reaps what he sows."

# 11

# Getting to the Bottom of Your Joy

JOHN PIPER

Several times I have asked a particular question at these Passion conferences. Let me give you the question and then tell you where we're headed with it in this chapter.

The question is, *Do you feel more loved by God when he makes much of you, or do you feel more loved by God when He frees you and enables you, at great cost to His Son's life, to enjoy making much of Him forever?*

Let me shorten it down so you can hear the essence of it. *Do you feel more loved by God because he makes much of you or because he enables you to make much of him?*

## Clearing Up a Misunderstanding

I've asked the question numerous times around the country, and what I have come to realize is that it has led to some significant misunderstandings that I hope to clear up here. So this chapter is designed to bring clarity and precision to that question, and what I mean by it, and what it doesn't mean.

Let me say it again. *Do you feel more loved by God because he makes much of you or because he, through Christ, enables you to enjoy making much of him forever?*

I think I have misled. For example, I think some people respond and say, "So Piper really doesn't believe that God makes much of us, or if he does, he doesn't think we should be happy about it or joyful in it because if we are happy that God makes much of us, then that contaminates our happiness in making much of him. That seems to be what Piper thinks."

That's not what I think. I don't want to mislead you. I don't want you to be left with unbiblical or disproportionate thoughts about these things. I want clarity. I want to be faithful to the Bible. What I'm after is biblical clarity and precision about what God is saying to us. It really doesn't matter in the end what I think. It matters what God thinks, and the only way we know what God thinks is because he has revealed himself to us, and what he thinks about a lot of things, in the Bible. And so all I care about, and all you should care about, is what does God think about this question I've been asking. What's God's answer to that question, or what should your answer be in God's eyes? I don't deny—indeed, I affirm with all my might—that God makes much of those who are in Christ. And we will come back to that shortly, and you will find things in the Bible that simply are beyond your imagination concerning how he makes much of you.

## Why Ask Such a Question?

So what am I trying to do with that question? If it's risky to ask a question like this one, which is open to misunderstanding, why would I use it? Why would I go around forcing this issue? *Do you feel more loved by God because he makes much of you or because he enables you to make much of him?*

I do it because I'm trying to help people. I'm trying to help you in this chapter exchange what's at the very bottom of your joy. I want you to exchange self at the bottom of your joy with God at the bottom of your joy. That's what I'm after in asking that question.

Let me clarify what I mean by "the bottom of your joy." I have a picture in my mind, and I hope you can keep it in yours in this chapter. All of our joys have a foundation, except one. Any happiness that you have in something has a foundation, except one. The one that has no foundation is the bottom.

## What's at the Bottom?

I'll give you an example. You make an A on a test, and it makes you very happy. That's understandable. I think that's a good thing. And somebody asks you, *Why are you happy about making an A on a test?* There could be many different answers. You can say, "It'll make mom and dad happy," or "I love the praise of my teachers," or, "It's going to be key in getting into graduate school in psychology." But then what if someone asks you, "Will just getting into graduate school make you happy?" And you might say, "Perhaps, because I've always had the dream of being a clinical psychologist, and I can't be one unless I go to graduate school in psychology. That's why the A leading to the graduate school makes me happy because then I can be what I've dreamed about being."

But then go deeper. Why do you want to be a clinical psychologist? Why does that make you happy? Why is this such a feeder for happiness? You might say, because you would love to help people, it makes you happy to think about the possibility of helping people by knowing them that way and giving God's perspective on how their mind works and their emotions work and their relationships work—that would make you happy.

So now, we're down about four levels. And then I would ask, Why does helping people make you happy? Now, we're getting close to the bottom, aren't we? And the bottom is where aren't any more answers. When you get to the bottom, you might say, "You just do." It's who you are. Where you end up as you penetrate down in your life to the bottom of what makes you happy is who you are. And there are two possibilities down there: making much of you or making much of God. And my hope in this chapter is to be used by the Holy Spirit to remove making much of self from the bottom and replace it with making much of God. Or you could simplify it as: self versus God.

Only you and God know your heart and how it's working right now and what makes you happy. There are so many layers of happiness, and they all have foundations. But one foundation has no foundation. And is that one foundation God or self? That's what my question is designed to illuminate.

## Is God Ultimate for You, or Self?

So let me ask it again. Do you feel more loved by God—or we could say, do you feel happier—because God makes much of you, or because God enables you to enjoy making much of him? I am not denying that God makes much of you, but I am forcing a ranking. I'm asking about the order at the bottom. When you get down to the bottom of your life, there is a ranking—either self is first, or God. I'm not denying that God makes much of us. It's a glorious thing to be enabled by the atoning blood of Jesus and the Holy Spirit to be freed from self and make much of God as your supreme joy and life, and it's a glorious thing to delight in being made much of by God. But everything hangs on their ordering, their ranking, they're being the bottom or not. That's what I'm after in this question. *Do you enjoy worshiping God, making much of God, because at the bottom, this God that you're worshiping is committed to making much of you?*

Do you enjoy worshiping God, making much of God, because underneath, at the bottom, he is committed to making much of you? That's idolatry of the worst kind. Or do you enjoy God's making much of you because it shows you the kind of God that He is? His making much of us enables us and equips us and transforms us so that we can actually see him for who he is and love him for who he is and treasure him for who he is and be satisfied in him for who he is. That's the bottom. Those are different people, different worlds, different destinies, that's what I'm after in that question. I want to hit people in the face with the deepest issue of their lives, that takes a miracle to change. That miracle is called the new birth.

## What It Means to Be Born Again

Why does this matter so much to me? Why is getting to the bottom of our joys such a big deal to me? I believe that there are perhaps millions of professing Christians who are not born again who believe God loves them and are hell bound, confident that they are loved by God and feeling it. That's why I ask that question, that's why it matters to me. Hundreds of you in this room perhaps feel loved by God but you're not born again, because what you mean by being loved by God is that at the bottom, He's committed to making much of you. He's not at the bottom, you're at the bottom and you don't want that, you don't want it short term, you don't want it long term. Millions of nominal Christians have never experienced the fundamental alteration in the foundation of that happiness.

To be born again—to be "regenerate," as the theologians have called it—is to experience at the bottom. The most fundamental thing that happens in the new birth is an exchange from myself as the source of all my joys, and myself being made much of, to God being the source of all my joys, and him being the bottom. Jesus becomes the supreme treasure. To know him and to make much of him becomes my deepest joy feeding all my other joys. In other words, all my fountains are in him. He has become the bottom. All my other desires, if I'm walking in him, are rising up out of that spring. He is the fountain from which all the other desires are coming. If there's any holiness in getting an A, it is because of him at the bottom.

I ask the question because, it seems to me, millions of nominal Christians are not born again. They haven't experienced this. Test yourself as I describe what is so tragically and fearfully true about so many. They have interpreted conversion to Jesus to mean that they can have all the same deepest desires they had before they were converted, only now the desires are met by another person, Jesus. So to get converted, for example, would mean that always if you always wanted to be wealthy and I've always sought it in the wrong places, now in Jesus there's a way to have what you've always wanted. Jesus is the way. He gives me what I always wanted: money. That's not new birth. You can sing to him till doomsday, jumping up and down, and it will not be anything pleasing to him.

Or you might have always wanted to be healthy. Now, instead

of going to all the doctors, you go to Jesus. "Did we not do many mighty works in your name?" some will one day ask Jesus. "Did we not cast out demons in your name? Did we not prophecy in your name? Did we not heal in your name?" And Jesus will say to them, "I never knew you. Depart from me workers of iniquity." That might be the most scary verse in the Bible! Miracles, prophecy, exorcism in Jesus's name, and they are hell bound. Do you think this is not an important question to ask?

What's at the bottom? So many professing Christians are on their way to destruction. Many of us would agree that wealth and health can be problems, but what if what you've always wanted is not to go to hell? And now, you hear one day, that there's a way not to suffer forever. His name is Jesus. "Yes, I don't want hell," you say, "so I'll take Jesus—since he's the way out of hell."

But what's at the bottom? Pain-free skin. No eternal suffering. But that's not the new birth. The new birth is not loving the same meal, but having a different butler. It's not having the same suitcases in your hotel room full of the same stuff, but with a different bellhop. That's not the new birth. The new birth is something new at the bottom. The suitcases at the bottom are different; the meal at the bottom is different.

## Helping You Have God at the Bottom

To become a Christian, in this way of seeing things (this bad way that I'm describing here) is to have all the same desires you have before you were born again, but now you just get them from a new place—and when you get them, you feel loved by God. That's very dangerous. So I'm asking, *Do you feel more loved by God if he makes much of you in all these ways, or have you experienced such a revolution in your heart that what is your deepest joy in your life is making much of God?* That's why I ask the question. The new birth changes the bottom, the root, the foundation of what makes us happy. Self at the bottom is replaced with Jesus at the bottom. This is why it matters to me so much. So I'm trying to help you put God at the bottom with his beauty and his value as your one deepest desire, feeding all your other desires, the fountain, the spring that explains everything you're happy about in life.

I'm not denying that God makes much of you. I want to affirm that with all my mind—and that's where we're headed. I want you to feel loved by God, but I'm so jealous that you not feel loved by God when he is not at the bottom. So then, let's ask this: *Why in the Bible does God perform all of his acts of love to us in such a way that the design of those acts of love is manifestly to make much of himself?*

## God's Design in Making Much of Us

Let me say that again. As I read my Bible, from beginning to end, and try to zero in on the places where it's really clear that God loves us, I'm amazed to discover what else God has to say in that context about why he's doing such acts of love. Does it terminate on me or on him? Does his loving me signify that I'm at the bottom, and that he's making my worth the foundation of everything, or is he doing it in such a way that it puts him at the bottom and makes his work the foundation of everything? My answer is that he always makes much of us in such a way as to make himself the bottom.

So I would like to give just a few examples this because you may not be familiar with the Bible enough to say, "Why can't I think of some text where that is true?" So let me illustrate what I mean when I say that throughout the Bible God loves us in such a way as to make clear that his design in loving us is that he would be made much of. His design in making much of us is to make clear that his goal is that he'd be made much of.

## God Shows His Love for Us by Adopting Us

First, Ephesians 1:5–6:

> In love he predestined us for adoption as sons through Jesus Christ, according to the purpose of his will, to the praise of his glorious grace . . .

God predestined us for adoption into his family. This happened before you were born. This is amazing love. And then there's this phrase: "to the praise of the glory of God's grace."

Why is God loving you into his family? Answer: So that you would spend your eternity making much of his grace. So there it is—this is the kind of thing I mean. It's all over the Bible—love towards me with the view toward making much of God. Whether you are wired to feel loved by is crucial to who you are. There are professing Christians all over the world, who would hear that and say, "I don't feel loved when you talk like that." Watch out.

So I'm asking, "Why does God talk like that?" He knows that some people are going to say, "I'm not feeling loved when you tell me that you're making much of me so that you get made much of. I'm not feeling loved by that." Why does he talk like this? I'll give you another text to illustrate.

## God Shows His Love for Us by Sending Us a Savior

Second, Luke 2:10–14:

> "Fear not, for behold, I bring you good news of great joy that will be for all the people. For unto you is born this day in the city of David a Savior, who is Christ the Lord. And this will be a sign for you: you will find a baby wrapped in swaddling cloths and lying in a manger." And suddenly there was with the angel a multitude of the heavenly host praising God and saying, "Glory to God in the highest, and on earth peace among those with whom he is pleased!"

Now, that's really something. A Savior has been born for sinners like me, and sinners like you. A Savior is born! I'm being loved on Christmas. I'm being pursued by God on Christmas. My sins will be forgiven, my guilt will be taken away, my condemnation will be renewed. God loves me and is after me.

So what do the angels say? *You are awesomely worthwhile.* That's not what they say. That's what we say if you're born again. We say, "Glory to God in the highest! I've been saved!" That's the way you talk when you're born again. You don't say, "What a good boy am I. or I'm a diamond in the rough—he bought me, you know. He's a good investor." You don't talk like that—not if you're born again. It's sad that there are Christians who talk like that. They say things like, "The cross is evidence of how valuable I am." But we should turn that right on its head—the cross is a manifestation of the unspeakable grace of God. We will spend eternity making much of God because he saved us.

So I'm loved *for his sake.* And when you're born again, that's the way you want it to be. The regenerate wouldn't have it any other way. They don't want to be at the bottom. They want his glory at the bottom—that's what it means to be born again.

There's far too many people who are all into God because they think God has made them the bottom.

## God Shows His Love for Us in the Death of Jesus

Third, 2 Corinthians 5:14–15:

> The love of Christ controls us, because we have concluded this: that one has died for all, therefore all have died; and he died for all, that those who live might no longer live for themselves but for him who for their sake died and was raised.

Was it for our sake? Yes. Was it for his glory? Yes. And everything hangs on *how* you get that right.

Are you glad to be died for, to be loved by the blood of Jesus, by the suffering Savior? Yes, we are. And why? This is what Paul says: "He died for all, that those who live might no longer live for themselves." I think that he means essentially "might no longer live with themselves at the bottom, needing to be made much of as the bottom and the source of all the joys, but rather now live for him who, for their sakes, died and was raised."

So the bottom of our joy is the glory of Christ in making much of Christ.

At one of the first Passion conferences in the late 90s, the title of my message was "Did Christ Die for Us or for God?" The answer to that question was, "Yes, He did die for us, but he died for us with a specific design that he manifests clearly in the Bible—that we would make much of him." That's his deepest goal—that's what's at the bottom and is ultimate.

## God Shows His Love for Us in the Way Jesus Prays for Us

Fourth is John 17, the longest prayer of Jesus in the Bible. You should feel greatly loved by this prayer. He's praying for you. He says in verse 20, "I do not ask for these only, but also for those who will believe in me through their word." And he's praying for us today as he did then. We should feel greatly loved. Jesus is praying for you, he's interceding for you, he's on your side. But listen to what he says in verse 24:

> Father, I desire that they also, whom you have given me, may be with me where I am, to see my glory that you have given me because you loved me before the foundation of the world.

So, what's he praying for me? He says, "Father, I love those who are in me by faith—those whom you have given me. And I'm asking this for them. My supreme request is that you cause them to be with me that they may see how glorious I am." That's what he's praying for you.

So, we ask, "Is this prayer for me or for him?" The born-again person is happy to say, "It's for me because it's for him. He is at the bottom and I'm resting on him. He's loving me, interceding for me, drawing me to himself because he is supremely valuable, and to see him and know him and enjoy him and show him is my greatest joy."

To be born again is to experience that—to hear John 17:24 and to say, "Yes!" Heaven isn't endless golf or endless virgins or endless health, but it's endless Jesus, seeing him, loving him, treasuring him, having him at the bottom as my greatest joy.

## Why Does God Do It This Way?

The reason I point to those four texts is simply to show you the tip of the iceberg that runs throughout the Bible. I could give you dozens more texts. They are all over the Scriptures. Throughout the Bible when God shows us his love for us, the surrounding contexts again and again show that he loves us with the specific design that he be made much of in and through and because of that act of love.

Now we ask, *Why does he do it this way?* Why does he do it this way when he knows that some people will feel unloved when that hear that he is loving us so that he gets the glory? Why does he do it this way?

Remember, I'm trying to answer and clarify the question, *Do you feel more loved by God because he makes much of you, or because he enables you to make much of him?* Before I give you the answer to why God talks like this, I am going to do what I've never done at Passion and give you seven ways that God makes so much of you. I do this because this is where I've been misunderstood—and perhaps rightly so. So this time it's different, and I want you to be blown away.

## How God Makes Much of Us

What follows is just Bible, and it's absolutely mindboggling. I ask the Holy Spirit to come in the next few minutes as you read through these texts and give you supernatural capacities to feel the truth and the wonder of what God says here, to the praise of Jesus's name. God makes much of all those who are in Jesus. *God makes much of you*, if you believe in Jesus, if you trust him, and he's your treasure and the bottom of your joy.

So, how does he make much of us who believe?

**1. God makes much of us by being pleased with us and commending our lives.**

One of C. S. Lewis' greatest sermons was called "The Weight of Glory." Reading it changed my life in 1968. There C. S. Lewis describes what he believes is the weight of glory that every Christian will gloriously bear: the words "Well done, good and faithful servant."

> To please God . . . to be a real ingredient in the divine happiness . . . to be loved by God, not merely pitied, but delighted in as an artist delights in his work or a father in a son—it seems impossible, a weight or burden of glory which our thoughts can hardly sustain. But so it is.[1]

I think Lewis is right.

Imagine you, a sinner, receiving this kind of commendation—from God. Some of you labor under the emotional burden that all you do is just displease God. Shortcomings everywhere. You don't read the Bible the way you should, or pray the way you should, or don't talk the way you should, or don't witness the way you should. You come to the end of everyday feeling, I'm hopeless.

Can you imagine that because of Christ, and your connection to him by faith, the Holy Spirit moves in your life, causes you to be born again, puts Jesus at the bottom, and God commits himself to say to you one day, "Well done, good and faithful servant"? God will say that to the thief on the cross who turned to Jesus. I don't think there's a select number of Christians that hear, "Well done!" while the rest get, "Lousy life. You basically blew it all the time, but you can come in anyway." I don't think anyone will hear that out of the mouth of Jesus at the last day. The thief on the cross who lived more than 99.9 percent of his life as a pagan and only half an hour as a born-again believer and heard from Jesus, "Today, you will be with me in paradise"—this same converted thief will hear Jesus say, "Well done!"

God makes much of us by being pleased with us through Jesus Christ.

**2. God makes much of us by making us fellow heirs with his Son who owns everything.**

God makes much of us by making you a fellow heir, an inheritor with His son who inherits everything in the universe. Here are some texts:

> Matthew 5:5: "Blessed are the meek, for they shall inherit the earth." Not just Atlanta, Georgia, or the United States, but all the planet, the whole Earth.
>
> Romans 4:13: "The promise to Abraham and his offspring [is] that he would be heir of the world."
>
> 1 Corinthians 3:21–23: "Let no one boast in men. For all things are yours, whether Paul or Apollos or Cephas or the world or life or death or the present or the future—all are yours, and you are Christ's, and Christ is God's." Francis Chan could probably

> illustrate this better than I. Perhaps he would set up some scales and put those statements on one side. "You Christian will inherit everything, everything. This is why I pray that you have the capacity to believe." He would say, "You live like that—it's out of sync. The scale is falling off the table. My life is not reflecting the kind of freedom from grumbling that you have when you're two seconds away from inheriting billions and billions of dollars, namely, the universe."

John Newton, who wrote "Amazing Grace," told this little parable about a man who was on his way to a big city to inherit a million dollars—which would be a whole lot more money today, let's just say $100 million. You're on your way to inherit $100 million, and you're riding in a horse-drawn carriage—we'll leave the carriage and not update that to a car—on your way happily to inherit $100 million You're not far away from the city, when a wheel falls off your carriage.

Here's a picture of our lives. We're not that far from home. This life is called a vapor's breath—like just two seconds. We'll call the broken carriage suffering, our light and momentary affliction. We're that close to our inheritance, we really are. Some reading this chapter will die this year; others, maybe 70 years out. But they're both virtually the same, and make little difference in light of eternity. It's that close, and then forever.

But Newton says that instead of running the rest of the way to get his inheritance, the man who has the broken wheel stumbles all the way into the city grumbling the whole way, "My chariot is broken, my chariot is broken." That's a picture of our lives. I see myself in that mirror, and I hate it. That's what Francis Chan meant when he said that our lives should be in accord with the gospel. The gospel has this in it. God makes much of us by granting us to inherit the world, and it's that far away—so why would you need to have it now?

Oh, Jesus makes much of you. Yes, he does.

**3. God makes much of us by having us sit at a table when Jesus returns, and he serves us as though he were a slave and we were the masters.**

Did you know that the Bible says that? I'll read it to you. It's from a parable in Luke 12:37:

> Blessed are those servants whom the master finds awake when he comes. Truly, I say to you, he will dress himself for service and have them recline at table, and he will come and serve them.

Not only is this what happened on the night before Jesus died, but also it will surely happen when he comes again, riding on a white horse, with a sword coming out of his mouth, as King of kings, Lord of lords, with "faithful" written on one thigh and "true" on the other, the mighty God himself. And once he sits on the throne and divides the nations, he comes down and finds himself with the towel and tells us, "Children, sit, sit," and he serves us.

Yes, you are made much of, and you will be made much of breathtakingly in that day.

**4. God makes much of us by appointing us to carry out the judgment of angels.**

How many angels are there? At least one hundred million. It says in Daniel 7:10 that "ten thousand times ten thousand stood before him." It may be lots more, but it's at least one hundred million.

When the apostles Paul is talking to this rag-tag ordinary

group disciples at Corinth, who can't figure out how to settle their own disputes, his argument for why they should be able to judge right and wrong, and settle their own disputes, is that they one day will be qualified to judge angels.

> When one of you has a grievance against another, does he dare go to law before the unrighteous instead of the saints? Or do you not know that the saints will judge the world? And if the world is to be judged by you, are you incompetent to try trivial cases? Do you not know that we are to judge angels? How much more, then, matters pertaining to this life! (1 Corinthians 6:1–3)

However, ordinary you may think you are, Paul would look into your face and say that you one day will judge angels. Now, I don't know what that involves. I just know this: it's not a small thing. He's not making little of you when he says that.

**5. God makes much of us by ascribing value to us and rejoicing over us as his treasured possession.**

Matthew 10:31:

> "Fear not, therefore; you are of more value than many sparrows."

Zephaniah 3:17:

> The LORD your God is in your midst,
> a mighty one who will save;
> he will rejoice over you with gladness;
> he will quiet you by his love;
> he will exult over you with loud singing.

If I hear that correctly, what he's saying is that in the last day, when God is done working on you, you will not simply be pleasing to God—you will be thrilling to God. I don't ever feel thrilling to God. I regularly feel like a failure in my sanctification. So I need all the help I can get from the Holy Spirit to believe Zephaniah 3:17, that one day, the love that God has for me now will come to a consummation in having so worked in me that he will look upon me and be thrilled. Here's another, Matthew 13:43:

> The righteous will shine like the sun in the kingdom of their Father.

I love that text. I've tried every now and then to look at the sun, and I can't. It will blind you if you look at the sun. So this text says, God's children, his people, one day will shine like the sun—which means nobody will be able to look at you with natural eyes. This is why C. S. Lewis says that one day people will be tempted to bow down and worship you, except that they will all be made perfectly holy, and they'll know better. But you will look like you're worthy of it because you will shine like the sun.

**6. God makes much of you by granting you to sit with Jesus on his throne.**

This is perhaps the most amazing one. This is Revelation 3:21, and Jesus is talking:

> The one who conquers, I will grant him to sit with me on my throne, as I also conquered and sat down with my Father on his throne.

That's scary. It sounds almost heretical. Is he going to put us on the throne of God? No, we won't go on the throne of God. Here's what I think it means, and God help me because I'm sure I don't get it all.

Paul says in Ephesians 1:23 that the church is "his body, the fullness of him who fills all in all." The universe is going to be filled with Jesus, and I think that probably means his manifest rule will extend, with no competitors, to the end of creation. And Ephesians 1:23 says that we are that fullness. I think this means something like sitting on the throne—that is, Jesus's rule will be exercised through us. He will share the rule of the universe with the likes of us.

## Yes, God Makes Much of Us—But Why?

So let it be said loud and clear now, as I close, that I do not deny, and never have denied, that God makes much of us. The question is ranking. Whether these amazing truths that ought to thrill our soul—and, yes, they should—are the very bottom of our joy or not. God makes much of us, and it should thrill our souls. But why? And if the answer is because you're at the bottom, and you love to be made much of, that's no evidence of being born again.

But if your answer is that God making much of me reveals more of God to me, and equips me to know him more, treasure him more, love him more, be satisfied in him more, then that is good evidence of being born again. That's the difference between the regenerate and the unregenerate: what's at the bottom.

## A Love That's Even Greater

Let's go back to the question I said I would try to answer, and then we're done. *Why does God all over the Bible reveal his acts of love toward us in a way that shows his design is that he get glory?* The answer is this: God's love for you that makes much of his glory is a greater love for you than if he made you your greatest treasure. God's loving you in such a way that makes him your supreme treasure is a greater love for you than if he made you your supreme treasure.

Why? Because self, no matter how glorious—and it one day will be glorious—can never satisfy a heart made for God. It feels so good to the fallen heart. It feels so good to have myself at the bottom and to be made much of. And until we're born again, we can't realize that self won't satisfy us. We will never be beautiful enough, strong enough, wise enough, admirable enough to be the bottom of our joy, and bear the weight of all the joy that you want for eternity. Self will not bear that weight. It will give way, and you will fall into the pit.

Only one thing can bear the weight of all the joy that you ache for forever: God.

God loves you. I want you to feel loved, as I close this chapter—and God wants you to feel loved. You are precious to him. You are *precious* to him. And the gift that he would want me to give you at the close of this chapter is to say this: "I love you, and you are so precious to me that I will not let your preciousness become your God. I will be your God. And I alone."

> *Father in heaven, I beg of you—for myself, my family, my five children, four daughters-in-law, 12 grandchildren, and for all those reading this chapter—I beg of you that you would put yourself at the bottom of our joys, that we would be born again, if we're not born again, and that we would be renewed, that you would relocate, O God, what's at the bottom. Get self and the making much*

*of self out and put yourself and making much of you in. Grant those reading right now a spiritual taste that many perhaps have never tasted before, namely, the awakening in their souls of true God-centeredness, and the awakening in their souls of having a God-exulting God at the bottom of their joys—a Christ-exulting Christ at the bottom of their joys. So grant that there would be an indomitable force in those reading. With you at the bottom, nothing can stop us. Nothing can daunt us. God, come and perform that miracle. I pray in Jesus' name. Amen.*

# 12

# Ready, Get Set, Go

JUDAH SMITH

I want to encourage you around the thought of community and the Church that Jesus is building around the world. Is that okay? Are you awake? You have to understand something, I get the privilege of pastoring a church in Seattle, but the way we do it, if I say something that you like, you can feel free to just say "amen." We've got an old lady in our church, and when I really get to preaching—when I really get going—she just stands up, crosses her arms, and makes a face that lets me know I'm really laying it down.

If you hear something you like, or something you don't like, just make a noise. Do something. We're engaging each other, correct? Then go with me to 1 Peter, chapter 2. But, first, a big hello from the home of the greatest NFL team . . . a big hello from the Seattle Seahawks. Yes, we're coming. Yeah, we're coming. Make no mistake. I know we're all up in the Georgia Dome right now, but Seattle's coming. Our rookie quarterbacks are coming, too. You don't want to see the Seahawks in the playoffs, okay Falcons? Okay, I'm just sayin'. I'm just sayin'. Let's come back together now.

1 Peter, chapter 2, and verse 1. If you're there, if you've got your Bible with you, that's great. If not, I think we've got it up on the screens for you to read along. 1 Peter, chapter 2, verse 1 says, "Therefore, laying aside all malice, all deceit, hypocrisy, envy and all evil speaking, as newborn babes desire the pure milk of the word that you may grow thereby. If indeed you have tasted that the Lord is gracious." Isn't that a great verse? That "you have tasted that the Lord is gracious."

"Coming to Him as to a living stone, rejected indeed by men, but chosen by God and precious. You also as living stones are being built up a spiritual house. A holy priesthood to offer up spiritual sacrifices acceptable to God through Jesus Christ." Therefore, it is also contained in the Scripture, quoting now from the prophet Isaiah, "Behold I lay in Zion a chief cornerstone, elect and precious. He who believes in Him will be by no means put to shame. Therefore, to you who believe He is precious. But to those who are disobedient, the stone which the builders rejected has become the chief corner stone and a stone of stumbling and a rock of offense. They stumble being disobedient to the word to which they were also appointed. But you, you are a chosen generation, a royal priesthood, a holy nation, His own special people that you may proclaim the praises of Him who called you out of darkness into His marvelous light."

Come on somebody! "Who once were not of people, but now are the people of God who have not obtained mercy, but now have obtained mercy." Come on now, this is our story! Can I hear an "amen?" I want to speak to you as I said a moment ago, around the thought and subject of the Church community. For lack of a better title, I'm going to title this talk "Ready, Get Set, Go." I want you to turn to your neighbor since we're getting verbally involved here this morning. I want you to turn to your neighbor on your right and say, "Ready." Come on everybody, get involved. "Ready." Turn to your other neighbor and say, "Get set." Then turn right back to your right and say, "Go." Yes there we go. Let's try it again. Turn to your other and ask "Ready?" Now to your other neighbor exclaim, "Get Set, Go!"

It's getting hot up in here! Hey, would you pray with me one more time? Ask the Holy Spirit . . . without the power and help of the Holy Spirit, we're not going to get very far this morning as we study the Word of God.

*Jesus we love You. Again, we come to You, Lord. We thank You that You hear us when we pray. We ask now by the power of the Holy Spirit that You would help us to see Jesus. To see Jesus in all of His beauty, His majesty, and His sufficiency. We love you God, and Lord while I have Your attention here, I would like to ask that You help the Seahawks beat the Falcons in the Super Bowl, in Jesus' name. And everybody say it . . . Amen.*

You ever seen a Shark Week? Have you ever watched Shark Week on the Discovery Channel? My motto is, "Let's live every week like shark week." I feel like we can change the world if we lived like every week was shark week. I love sharks. I'm obsessed with sharks. Shark Week is a big week in my life every year.

This last year of Shark Week, I wasn't able to access all the programming, but there was one afternoon I sat down on the couch, and flipped on the Discovery Channel and it was a fascinating program. They were studying great white sharks off the coast of Cape Town. I love great white sharks. I hate them, but I also love them. I'm watching the program, and I don't know what it is about

Shark Week hosts, but they all yell when they're hosting. Have you noticed this?

I'm just casually flipping on the Discovery Channel, wondering if this program is going to be engaging, but before I know it, I am so engrossed in the moment because these Discovery Channel hosts are just genius. They're preachers for crying out loud! The guy's on there and instantly, I'm glued to the television as he's screaming at me. He's like:

> "Ladies and gentlemen, welcome. We're in a boat right now off the coast of Cape Town. We've just put Sean in the water. There's blood everywhere. Great white sharks are circling the boat and we're going to test a theory today that single preys are far more likely to be attacked by great white sharks than a pack of prey. What we're going to do right now, we're going to put a single decoy seal, way afar from the boat, and then we're going to put a pack of seals together, and we're going to see if the great white shark gets the single seal more than the pack of seals."

Naturally, I'm engaged. I like volume. I have to admit, I like volume. It's amazing.

They literally have these rubber seals. It's just the silhouette of a seal and it's a piece of rubber and they put a whole cluster together. Then one lonely little rubber seal goes far into the distance in the camera shot and we wait. Thank God for editing. How long did they have to wait? We don't know. Sure enough, before you know it, ain't nothing like a great white shark in Cape Town.

That great white comes out of the water, almost its entire body, comes out of the water, it destroys this fake, rubber little seal. And the climactic conclusion of the Shark Week show is the host holding up a mangled piece of rope with dangling little remains of rubber. He's holding it up on the string; he's like, "Just as we suspected . . . it seems very obvious to us that if you are in shark infested waters, you ought to stay together in the pack and you will be far less likely to be attacked." And the credits roll.

I don't mean to overstate what I have just shared with you, but I might have just saved your life. To God be the glory. It is what it is. I just saved your life. It's funny because if I was ever around shark infested waters, I don't think I'd get in at all. But I guess if I'm going to get in, I want to get in with a bunch of you. Then I don't have to outswim the great white. I guess I'd just have to outswim you.

I don't think it's by chance. I don't think it's strange that even in nature, we're pointed to the power and significance of community. All you've got to do is turn on the Discovery Channel and before long you see some indicator, some arrow pointing us to the power, significance, and validity of community.

Can you remember the first time you read your Bible? Can you remember back that far? Some of you have been saved forever; some of you just recently. I was probably about eight or nine years old. But I really started reading my Bible more like when I was sixteen. I grew up as a pastor's kid. To be honest, as far as we can tell, I'm the seventh generation preacher in our family. [crowd claps] No, don't clap. Pray for the Smiths. We've got issues, okay. That's all that means.

I remember reading Genesis 1 for the first time. Have you all ever read Genesis 1? God is, well, He's talking to Himself. He says in Genesis 1:26, "Let us make man in our image." For those of you that are not scholars, you're wondering what I wondered. *Wait a minute. Who's us? And whose our?* "Our image" . . . it's like . . . Hello? Anybody there? God, I know this is awkward, but who are You talking to? I mean You're God; I suppose You can talk to

Yourself, and if You want an alter ego, You could create it I suppose. Who are You talking to? "Let us make man in our image."

For those of you that are so scholarly and you've been around the Church for so long, you're like, "Clearly, that is a reference to the triune Godhead." For the rest of us that watch NFL games and live real life, it's a bit confusing. If you ever catch me by myself, referring to myself as "us and our and we," get me to the doctor as fast as you can.

Obviously, it's true, the scholarly amongst us are right. What God is referencing is Himself. For we serve a God who is one God, but three persons. I don't mean to lose you right off the bat here this morning, but I know you're with me. We serve a God who is singular in character and nature, but plural in person. We serve God the Father, God the Son, and God the Holy Spirit. This is our God. This is the God we sing to. This is the God we preach about. This is the God we pray to. This is the God we think about often. This is God the Father, the Son, the Holy Spirit. He is beautifully three-in-one—distinguishable, but indivisible.

"Let us" . . . Father, Son, Holy Spirit . . . "make man in our" . . . Father, Son, Holy Spirit . . . "image." How important is community to God? Wait a minute. God *is* a community, in and of Himself.

While we're on the subject . . . so that brings us back to the verse I just quoted, "Let us make man in our image." We are made in the image of *who*? Our God. We are made in the image of our God; Our God who within Himself is a community—distinguishable, indivisible, singular in nature and character, but plural in person. Our God, who *is* a community, we are created in His image.

We are community beings, designed for community. You are not an isolated individual living in close proximity to others. You are an interconnected, interdependent being, intended for relationship and intimacy. The Bible says in Proverbs that the man who isolates himself seeks his own desires and rages against all wise judgment. *He rages.* God has intended each and every one of us to live within community.

I can prove to you how important relationship and community are, and of course, when we speak of this concept of community that is the essence of the Church. This term we throw around now and have for centuries, this word *Church* is really a community that centers around Jesus. When we say *Church*, we are also saying *community.* So when we say *community*, we also are saying *Church*, in a sense.

I can prove to you how imperative community is. In the beginning, back to Genesis, everything's perfect, right? God's made Adam. Everything's awesome. He's got pets galore. He's got waterfront property. He's got organic food, organic sugar. It's awesome. Everything is pretty amazing. You know in all of the perfection of Eden and Adam's initial existence, God says there was one thing that's not good. Everything is perfect—friends, sinless, perfect. But God says, "Wait. One thing is not good. Adam's by himself." And this is where all the men said, "Amen!"

It's not good. I want you to hear the words of your God this morning. If you're alone, it's not good. You may be saying, "Well, Judah, it's not my fault." And that is true. There are people in this room—your aloneness, your isolation, your loneliness is not even of your own doing. But it remains. The truth remains that it is not good for mankind to be alone. We are designed for community, for we are designed in the image of a God, who within Himself, is a community.

Now that we've laid that in place, we'll pick up on where we left off there in a moment. I want us to ask a great cosmic question.

Any time you ask a really deep cosmic question you should ask it in breathy tones, because that note is true. This is true. It will help you ponder more appropriately. We're going to ask the question, "What is man's all?" We're going to do it in a much more profound, meaningful way. Something like this: "What is man's all-all-all . . . ?" [the word *all* echos] Do you feel that though? I feel reflective the moment I say it like that. "What is man's all?" [echoing words] Do you feel that? I feel that.

What is man's all? It's a pretty appropriate question at high noon here in Atlanta, Georgia. What is man's all? To live? To eat? How many feel like it's eat? Hello! To breathe? To love? To sing? To dance? What is man's all? It brings us back to Genesis. Man's all is very simple. It is to reflect the image of its Creator. This is mankind's all. It sounds like by the few claps we've heard, there is a remnant in this place that agrees with my premise. [laughs]

What is man's all? To reflect the image of our God. This is our passion. This is where we find our greatest fulfillment. This is where we find our truest meaning when we reflect the image of our Creator. Creation . . . all of creation, and even creation's centerpiece, which is mankind. All of creation finds its proper place and meaning and positioning and purpose when it accurately reflects the image of the Creator. This is our passion.

Having established that, and having just a few moments ago established that we serve the great Three-In-One, we must conclude, my brothers and sisters, that it is impossible to fulfill "man's all" alone. For God, within Himself, is Father, Son, and Spirit. If mankind is going to reflect the Creator in an accurate way, majestic in the truest sense we possibly can, we must conclude today, here in Atlanta, Georgia, that it is impossible to fulfill our ultimate purpose and plan in this life alone.

The fact is I need you, as awkward as it is to admit. Some of you, I don't like you, you falcon fans, but . . . don't cheer. But I need you. And this is my favorite part. You need me. [chuckles] My Seahawk-loving self, you need me. We need each other. I'll ask you a simple question this morning: What is more important than the world seeing God? What is more important than the world seeing the beauty and the majesty and the sufficiency of our Savior? What is more important than that?

There is nothing more important. If that is of the highest importance, then what urgency does that place on our interconnectedness and our commitment to community, and relationship, and love, and respect, and honor one to another. Friends, simply put, without community, our world will not see God.

Why do I love the Church in all of her beautiful forms, and all of her uniqueness and frankly at times, bizarreness? Because without God's community on the planet, God's planet may never see Him. I love Church because I love God. I love God and I love what He loves, and what He loves is this planet. He loves this planet so much, He gave this planet a gift—His Son, who established a community where within the world could look and see the image and a portrait of His beauty and His Majesty, His essence. [crowd cheers] Thank you. I'll take that "amen" for the next few minutes emotionally. Thank you.

1 Peter, chapter 2, gives a really interesting metaphor on who we are. And you noticed 1 Peter, 2; we read ten verses there and we don't have time to read all of the context and everything. But did you catch that? God says . . . He inspires Peter to write this letter . . . and then He says, "Let's see. People are like? What are people like? People are like living stones. That's what they're like."

I know if I was choosing the metaphor to describe humanity, I'd want something a little bit more than a rock. Like really, building material is the best metaphor that you can come up with God? How about a cheetah? How about a boa constrictor? Anything's better than a rock. While we're on topic, how about the guy who created the concept of "pet rock?" That guy's the smartest guy, by the way. That guy rocks. Sorry, too easy . . . too easy. Move on, move on.

Really? God, a rock? He's like, "Okay, Peter, write this down. My people are like living rocks, though—not dead ones—alive ones." Great. It's awesome. Thanks. Could I be an eagle? Could I be a falcon? *No, you may never be a falcon.* That was the Lord saying that to me. *Falcons are bad my child.*

It is interesting, right? Peter's writing about those who are redeemed, those who are added into the redeemed and the saved; those who are purchased by Jesus, who put their faith in Him. He says, "I'll tell you what you're like. You're like a building material, is what you're like. You're like living, breathing building material." [laughs]

It's very clear to me that God intends to build something with our lives. It seems to me that every salvation is a new stone admitted to a building program in God's plan on this planet. There are a lot of rocks that you walked by this morning on your way into this dome. There are. Not one person here this morning walked in from your hotel or wherever you are staying, and you saw a pebble or a bit of a larger rock and you stopped, and you were like, "Stop. Everyone . . . are you seeing what I'm saying?" *No, dude, I don't. What?* "Look at this." *Hey man, what are you looking at?* "You don't see what I see? It's a rock, man. I've never seen anything like it." *Hey man, are you on something, man? I know it's legal in Seattle, but not here brother.* [crowd laughs] Too soon? I apologize. Too soon, too soon.

No, that never happened. Nobody walked in flabbergasted over one singular rock. I don't know about you, but when I walked in here this morning and looked around this building, and the people in it are of most value, but I must admit when it comes to rocks, this is one of my favorite collections. You look around this dome and it is awe-inspiring. Friends, essentially all this dome is, is a bunch of little rocks that got together and together it builds one of the buildings that's a wonder in this world.

Let us not miss the message, the significance, the imperativeness of community. When we get together, and let's be honest, getting together is not always easy, trusting leadership, faulty leaders that are not perfect. Going to a local place, being with people who know your name, who know where you live, doing life together, studying the Bible together, challenging one another. People who call you when you're not seen or heard from for some time. Sometimes being connected is flat annoying. "Leave me alone. You don't know me." Before long, we want to do our own thing. Friends, if the world is going to be in awe of the image of our Savior, and our King, and our God, we must get together. We've got to stay connected. It is imperative.

So far I think we've answered what God is building on the planet. I've touched a little bit on why He's building it on the planet, and I'd like to conclude in the last few moments we have, with *how?* How do we get connected? How do we stay connected? What makes our community different than other communities on the planet?

Let's be honest, there's all kinds of cute communities popping up in our Western world and for those that are in other parts of the world, they're proliferating everywhere, aren't they? We've got little communities around our local grocery store. We've got online communities. We've got sports communities. We've got all kinds of communities that are on the basis of caffeine. Communities on the basis of raw sugar. Communities on the basis of eleven guys they don't even know, but they run around with a piece of pig so they all gather around those eleven men they'll never know, but they idolize that. We've got all kinds of communities. Wait a minute . . . What makes the Church different than any other community? That's a good question, a fair question, an honest question. In the same way that you and I are called living stones in 1 Peter, chapter 2, Jesus is called the Living Stone. Jesus is called the Living Stone, now that's an interesting metaphor to use in reference to God's Son as well because once again, it's very clear in Scripture that God intends to build something genuine, authentic, real, and tangible in terms of people around His Son.

Jesus is building something on this planet. He's not just here to individually save people. And of course, He is, but those individuals are to be added to a collection that makes up His portrait and His picture on the planet. God is building something, but it must be built around the Living Stone.

Someone asked me recently, "What's your best definition of grace?" We want a definition on grace? It seems pretty simple to me. I said, "Jesus." *What do you mean?* "You want my best definition of grace, right? That's what you asked? Not just a definition, but my best. Well, it's Jesus."

*What's your best definition of love?* "Jesus." *What's your best definition of integrity?* "That would be Jesus." *What's your best definition of faithfulness?* "My best? You just want my, not . . . oh, Jesus." *Okay, what's your best definition of . . .* "I'm going to give you the same answer, it's Jesus." *What do you mean?* "Wait a minute . . . What do you mean?"

Wait . . . did you think this book was about a collection of principles and moral concepts? Did you think that the Church of

Jesus Christ is a collection of informed people who are adhering to some list of concepts, and morality, and discipline, and devotion; that somehow we're just disciplined people and we just adhere to a certain code? Wait a minute, what do you mean?

Define grace. Define love. Define mercy. Define faithfulness. Define self-control. Define integrity. *What do you mean define it?* It's all Jesus! This book is not a mere collection of principles, concepts, or moral attributes. This is a story, and it's about a person, and His name is Jesus, and if you're looking for love, or if you're looking for grace, or if you're looking for goodness—you can find it in Him.

Let's be careful students that we're not busy adhering to a code or concepts or principles and we miss the person. It's all about Jesus. I love 1 Peter 2 because multiple times it uses this word *precious.* He's precious. He's the most precious person in the world. What makes our community transcendent above all other communities on the planet? It is not our lights. It is not our showmanship. It is not our talent. It is not our abilities. It is not our wherewithal, our knowledge. It's not. What makes us different than any other gathering in the world? There's only one . . . one person, one Savior, one sinless, perfect God-man and Him alone is what brings us together and keeps us together and makes us a peculiar people on this planet. It's Jesus. It's Jesus. It's Jesus!

I grew up playing sports, and playing basketball at my high school. I learned that good coaching is all about assessing your players. We had a 6 foot 11, 275 pound center my senior year of high school. That was the same year your Passion Conference started. I'm sorry Louie. I was so young. Guess what we did at Issaquah High School? Guess who got the ball almost every time down the floor? Jason Heidi. Why? Because he's 6 foot 11, 275 pounds.

I remember one time my coach said, "Gentlemen, look around. Look around the locker room." He's like, "What do you see?" He says, "I'll tell you what you see. You see only one man in here who's 6'11, 275 pounds. That's what you see." He said, "Judah, how tall are you?" I said, "On paper or in real life, coach? You listed me at 6'4, but I'm 6'1 and 1/2." He said, "How much do you weigh?" I said, "178." He said, "Thank you." He went around, literally . . . this happened. Coach Moscatello . . . this happened.

He said, "Think about it gentlemen. There's no other guy that's 6'11, 275 pounds in this league." He said, "By the way, Coach K and all these great, famous coaches that are coming to our game, no offense Judah, but they're not here to see you. They came to see Jason. Why? He's 6 foot 11, 275 pounds, Judah. He's twice the man you are."

He's got a good point. If you're going to win, you play to your strength. You look at the inventory of your team and you go, "Oh, the coaches are coming to see him. He's the biggest. He's the fastest. He's the strongest." Church can we, for a moment, stop, be honest, look around and go, "We're pretty average. We're pretty ordinary, extraordinary in our value and worth before God, but average and ordinary in our humanness." Before long, you turn and you realize there is one amongst us and 6'11, 275, would not even begin to describe His girth, His majesty, His beauty, His glory, His sufficiency. [laughs]

Jesus is enough. If we'll make Him a big deal, if we'll make Him most important, the MVP of our life and our gatherings and our communities, we will be sticky. We will be effective. We will be transcendent. We will be unique. We will be peculiar on this planet, and there is coming a day, and the day has already begun, where the world is taking notice from coast to coast, from continent to continent. The nations are rising and standing and they're declaring there is a God. He's beautiful. He's wonderful and He's alive. Come on, you and me. Let's get together. Let's stay together and let's make Jesus a big deal. If you believe that, somebody shout amen!

*For more from Judah Smith go to thecity.org*

# 13

# Fearless

LOUIE GIGLIO

Every Passion gathering has moments that get etched into our story for a long, long time. These are like snapshots of what God was doing in our midst at a given moment—pictures that capture the heartbeat of what's happening in this movement. I remember, for example, in 2012 when one of our volunteers, our Door Holders, told me a story about Tikki, one of the supervisors of the custodial staff in the Georgia World Congress Center where we were holding part of the event. Tikki had come to our volunteer and pointedly asked with some bewilderment, "What's going on here?" She knew a conference was going on, so the question was about more than an event. Tikki was asking a deeper question. She was feeling something inside her that she'd never felt before. During that conversation, our Door Holder was able to share with her about the grace of Jesus. In the end, that searching venue custodian, whose responsibility it was to make sure the building was in order, suddenly came face to face with the God of the universe.

I remember at that same event when we were singing "How Great is Our God" at the top of our lungs, how that song started to trend number one on Twitter worldwide. Now I don't know how many people it takes to get something to trend number one in the entire world, but I'm assuming it's a bunch. And out of an arena in Atlanta, Georgia, the hashtag #HowGreatIsOurGod was showing up on people's mobile devices and computers around the globe. Maybe it's just a little thing, but for me it was a picture of the impact a generation can make when everyone plays their part as they lean the same direction for a common cause.

Those are just two different examples, one on a local level and one on a worldwide scale, of the end result of what you find in Luke 7 after Jesus raised a young man back to life. When Jesus starts interrupting the funerals in people's lives, the matter doesn't stay private. The end result is the same now as it was then: the news of Jesus spread all throughout the country. When Jesus touches your life like no one else can, the domino effect is that you become a part of the "big picture" plan of God—namely, that His name and His fame spread far and wide.

And that's something you can be a part of right now if you want. God is inviting you into the incredible process of championing His name in your generation. Unfortunately, though, most of us have been hardwired by the world's way of thinking into believing that taking hold of that message is some distant reality out in our future somewhere. Often we think being powerfully used by God is a "someday" thing instead of a "right now" thing. We live in holding-pattern thinking that sets us up for a "not yet arrived" mentality, always waiting for what comes next instead of taking hold of the right now.

This pattern is built into us very early in life, especially in the

United States. When you are in middle school, you're constantly thinking about what life is going to be like when you get to high school. Once you get to high school, you get a bit of a pass during your freshman and sophomore year, but when you become a junior, you've got to start thinking about college. You've got to make sure your GPA is right, and you start taking the prep courses for the standardized testing. When you get to be a senior, you get asked at least twenty times a week where you're going to go to college. Everyone wants to know what you're going to do when you graduate.

Then, when you finish high school and if you do attend college, you start getting hammered with questions about your major. Then come the questions about internships, summer activities, and grad school. As you get closer to earning your degree, the questions start getting really tough, because now they're focused not just on education but on career:

"What are you going to be?"

"What are you going to do?"

"Have you looked into the job market?"

"How much does that pay?"

At that point, you have the same answer you did when you were in middle school: it's a mixture of exasperation and anxiety, because the truth is you just don't know. And with every step, you shift your thinking to the future, saying to yourself, *If I can just make it to high school. If I can just make it to college. If I can just make it to my degree.*

The really bad news is that it doesn't change that much when you get out of school. After you get into a job, you start thinking about the next job. And then there's the family aspect, and now you're wondering about getting married, having kids, and moving into a house. Then the cycle starts all over again as you start asking the same questions about your kids that were asked of you.

It's a system of a not-yet-realized future opportunity that supposedly will eventually come. It's always later, later, later. But here's the thing: when you come alive in Jesus Christ, your mission and purpose doesn't begin someday. It begins now!

That doesn't mean that your story doesn't unfold to greater and more varied opportunities; it does. It just means that you don't have to constantly be waiting for what's coming next to fully participate in the purposes and plans of God. They are right now. And you only have to be afraid of one thing—not having your life count for what really matters. You don't have to fear getting it wrong or missing "God's will" if you just stay connected to Jesus in the "right now."

We see this *right now* way of life in what the Apostle Paul wrote in Ephesians 6:19–20:

> Pray also for me, that whenever I speak, words may be given me so that I will fearlessly make known the mystery of the gospel, for which I am an ambassador in chains. Pray that I may declare it fearlessly, as I should.

What a prayer! I wonder if we lumped together thousands of our prayers from today into one big heap if anywhere in there would be the cry, "God, just use me under any circumstances to fearlessly make known your name."

And here's what makes this prayer from Paul even more meaningful: he's not writing it from his back veranda with a stunning sunset view. He's not lounging on a couch with a latte, brainstorming out some ideas for the church at Ephesus. He's not sprawled out on the dorm room floor of a friend. He's a prisoner in a Roman jail, chained to the wall. Paul has been arrested and imprisoned for his boldness in sharing the message of Jesus. So this hand, writing this prayer, is *literally* bound, and yet this is what he asks for.

It would have been so easy for Paul to ask the Ephesians to pray that he would be released. That the magistrate would have a softened heart. That his trial would go well. That there would be another earthquake like there was in Philippi and he would miraculously escape. But he doesn't. He doesn't focus on his circumstances; he focuses on the message of the gospel. He focuses on what matters most. Paul doesn't ask God for a way out. He asks God to give him boldness to get the message out.

Paul wasn't waiting for something to change in his life. He wasn't looking to some not-yet-realized opportunity in the future when things would be different than they were at that moment. He was thinking about now. And I've got to wonder what might happen if you and I did the same thing.

What would happen if you moved this prayer of Paul to the top of your prayer list? What would happen if you spent as much energy praying for fearlessness to make known the gospel as you do for your circumstances to change? What would happen if each of us took hold of the opportunities before us rather than waiting for something else to come our way in the future?

To be honest, there are a couple of big hurdles to this kind of praying. These hurdles can keep us in the holding pattern, waiting on the future, instead of moving into the plans and purposes of God right now. If you want to move this prayer of Paul to the top of your prayer list, then you are going to have to trust Jesus to help you overcome these things.

The first hurdle is one that I would broadly call brokenness.

That can mean a lot of different things: adversity, trial, hardship, a season of life that feels like it's going to snap you in half, or whatever is making your life a mess right now. It could be a wound from the past or a present circumstance. That's a significant hurdle because when you're living in the middle of brokenness, it's often all you can see. Your focus is on what's wrong, and you're spending all your time and energy looking at what's broken. I get that; I've been there in my story, too.

In 1995, Shelley and I were living in Waco, Texas, where for ten years we had been walking with students at Baylor University every day. We had seen God do amazing things, and we were excited about the future. But for seven of those years, my dad had been disabled in Atlanta, Georgia. He had gone from being completely healthy physically, and a brilliant artist and graphic designer, to being an invalid because of a brain virus. My sister, mom, Shelley, and I were living in one of the darkest tunnels you can imagine. So Shelley and I made the difficult decision to leave Texas and our ministry there and move to Atlanta to be involved in the twenty-four-hour-a-day process of caring for my father. Then, just before we arrived in Atlanta, my father died.

We had left everything to move there, confident that it was the right yet difficult decision for us to make. Then, all of a sudden there was no dad and no ministry, and we were left wondering what happened. What we found was through that process of pain God had loosened our grip on what we thought was possible and moved us into a position of total flexibility and availability to Him. We began to hear the voice of the Lord speak in a clearer way about the future of Passion than we ever dreamed.

Now imagine, fifteen years after that, walking into the Georgia Dome where we have held Passion events and looking down onto the football field where the Chick-fil-A Bowl was going to be played only twenty-four hours before a Passion gathering of thousands of college students was going to be held. I walked into that dome and saw painted on the middle of the field the logo for Chick-fil-A (that's a fast-food chicken restaurant for those of you who don't live in cities graced with a location). It's the same logo that was designed in 1964; the same one they paid a designer seventy-five dollars to create. It's the same logo that has endured seven different ad agencies, all of which wanted to change it. And the designer of that logo . . . Louie Giglio, my dad.

Here I was, in the Georgia Dome a few nights before our first stadium gathering. And I was standing on the field next to my dad's design—a design painted below where our stage would be set. God had brought me back together with my dad, reminding me He had used my time of confusion and heartache to move me exactly where He wanted me to be. God saw the path all along and knew that my dad's illness and death would be the doorway through which Passion would arrive. The point is this: brokenness is the bow from which God launches arrows of healing.

It's true of me, and it can be true of you. It was certainly true of Paul. That same hand that wrote Ephesians 6 with chains around its wrist wrote these words in Philippians 1:

> Now I want you to know, brothers and sisters, that what has happened to me has actually served to advance the gospel. As a result, it has become clear throughout the whole palace guard and to everyone else that I am in chains for Christ. And because of my chains, most of the brothers and sisters have become confident in the Lord and dare all the more to proclaim the gospel without fear. (vv. 12–14)

Here we see again the apostle, confined by a prison cell, but not waiting for circumstances to change before he jumps headlong into the purposes of God. Instead, we see Paul looking around at his mess and embracing what God can do right in the middle of it.

He's in jail? No sweat. Must be time for prisoners and guards to hear the gospel.

He's being persecuted? Perfect. What a great chance for others to be encouraged to live fearlessly for the sake of Jesus.

Don't let the enemy tell you that your broken situation disqualifies you from being a part of the news of Jesus spreading throughout the country. It doesn't. Brokenness is the bow from which God launches arrows of healing to the world that lives in a mess. For of our Lord it is said, "By His wounds, we are healed."

I think the second hurdle for people embracing the right now and joining the plans and purposes of God is that they feel like they just don't know what to do. In fact, many of us know the paralysis that comes with being unsure about whether or not we really know what God's will for our lives is. But there is another path. Sometimes I wish we could just remove the question "What is God's will for my life?" from our vocabulary. It's not that the question is bad; you should care an awful lot about what God's will is for your life. The problem is when we ask it so much that it becomes a hurdle to actually living in the middle of what God has already told us *is* His will for our lives. Paul tells us at least part of what God's will is, and he asks us to move it to the top of our prayer list: "Pray for me that when I speak, God will give me the words to proclaim fearlessly the mystery of the gospel."

That is the will of God for you regardless of where you are. You're in the computer lab? You're in a suburb? You're sitting at your desk? You're changing a diaper of a two-year-old? Great. Go for it. In your bank, in your hospital, in your neighborhood, on your team, wherever it is that you find yourself, fearlessly proclaim the mystery of the gospel. When you start doing that, you will find all the other questions you might have about the will of God for your life suddenly don't seem that pressing anymore. That's because you've come to realize that wherever you are, and whatever you're doing, you know the real reason God has placed you in that moment: to fearlessly proclaim the news about Jesus.

We can't wait until every single detail is clarified and all our questions are thoroughly answered to move into the future. We can't wait until all the brokenness goes away. We can't wait until we've got a handwritten message in the sky from God telling us which apartment complex to live in. We can take hold of the purposes of God, and we can do so without fear.

That's really what's left, isn't it? You overcome the hurdle of brokenness. You overcome the hurdle of not knowing what to do, and then the only thing holding you back is fear. Your fear of failing. Your fear of what will happen in the future. Your fear of your past. Your fear of not finding a job. Your fear of not having the kind of life you always dreamed you would. Your fear of being single. Your fear of being married.

Maybe the big fear for you is the fear that you're never going to be valued. That's driving your fear of being alone and your fear of losing your job. Maybe your big fear is about security, that you're never going to be safe. That's why you're constantly worried about money, and that's why you can't ever seem to have enough. How do you conquer these fears?

You do it by reducing all those fears to one fear—the fear of living an insignificant life. That may sound confusing at first, but let me explain. For most of us fear will always try to find a seat at our table. Try as we may, we can't keep it away. But we can do something; we can give that seat at the table to something else. We can replace that seat with confidence that God is bigger than whatever we are unsure of. And we can replace the fear of a thousand things with the fear of one. Our freedom will come—even in a prison cell—when our main objective is to not live life without making the message of Jesus known. If you are convinced that making His fame known is the nonnegotiable of your life, you will overcome every other obstacle, viewing the challenges you face as avenues to tell His story, not a hindrance to your story.

And the first person you declare the message of Jesus to is yourself.

You stand in the face of all other fears and tell them, "Jesus died for me. I am valued. Jesus is holding me. I am secure. Jesus loves me. I am significant." You fearlessly proclaim that message to yourself over and over again, and suddenly you start to find all the rest of the fears being crushed under the mighty name and power of Jesus Christ. And in that conviction about your own worth and freedom you speak up to the world.

Boldness doesn't come from trying to be bold. It comes from being convinced of who and whose you are. To be fearless isn't necessarily to be loud, but to be sure. It doesn't mean that you stand and shout at the world, but that you walk with a glow they can't deny. And no argument from those trying to discredit the faith can slow you down. Once you've heard Jesus' voice speak freedom over your life, what can stop you from standing unmoved in that freedom whether we you are in a prison cell or a privileged place? Once you realize that you are made whole in His love, even your wounds become a beacon for the hands that hold you. Fear is replaced by fearless as the world looks on. Jesus trumps the chains that try to bind us and, as a result, the message of grace echoes freely throughout our world.

So what circumstances, fears, or wounds are keeping you from believing that you are brand new by faith in Christ right where you are? What is trying to chain you down and hold you back? Take a step back and ask God to help you see what He sees. Ask Him to help you see yourself as someone He dearly loves and has purposefully chosen. And ask Him to give you His vantage point on the circumstances around you. You'll see that jail cells and binding chains are nothing to the God who flung the stars into space. All you have to do is open your hands to Jesus and ask Him to use you. And when you do, get ready. "Jesus, use me" is a prayer He always answers.

14

# Living a Life That Makes Sense

FRANCIS CHAN

I love my wife. She is absolutely amazing, and we have an incredible marriage. But just before this last Christmas, we ran into a little problem.

Christmas was approaching, and I was trying to figure out what to get her. I started thinking about this old minivan that she drives. I mean, this van is so old that the paint is just peeling all over the place. I'm not joking. We'll be driving down the road and the paint will literally flake off. And then there's the reality that we have five children. That's a lot of kids! So we have a family of seven, and our minivan holds seven. Plus we sometimes think about adopting more, so we could easily be outgrowing the minivan soon. We had talked about replacing it. We wanted to get rid of it before it died on us, and we probably needed something bigger.

All of this was going through my mind, and I began to think, *You know what? I'm going to surprise her. I'm going to get her a new car for Christmas. That's romantic, isn't it? I've seen those commercials where the wife gets a new car with a huge bow on the hood. It's beautiful! I'm doing that!*

So I started my search. I was checking out those giant people-mover vans that youth groups and huge families use. I looked at Honda Pilots, Honda Odysseys, and Toyota Siennas. I talked to friends who own car dealerships and asked them to keep an eye open for the right car at the right price. I did all of this legwork because I love my wife and she's worth it.

And then the moment came when I had to decide. Which car was I going to get her? That's when I froze. What if I picked the wrong car? I really wanted to surprise her. I wanted her to walk outside to the car with the bow on the hood, just like in the commercial. But I couldn't pull the trigger without asking her.

So a couple of days before Christmas, I confessed to her. I said, "Honey, I don't know what to do with your Christmas present. I'm getting you a big old present." As soon as I said it, she got visibly excited. I was feeling so good about myself. I continued, "But I have to ask you to help pick the right one because I don't want to mess this up." She was still excited. She started asking, "What? What? What!" So I spoiled the surprise: "I'm getting you a car!"

And that's when her face fell. She looked at me and said, "That's not a present."

"What? What do you mean? How is that not a present?"

"Well," she said, "we've already talked about getting a car and we decided that we need one. So that's a necessity. Not a present."

Later on I got a pseudo-apology from her in a text message. She said, "Sorry to burst your bubble, honey. But a girl does not consider a car to be a present." Apparently a present is something you don't really need. Maybe it worked for the lady in the commercial because she didn't need a brand new Lexus. But now my surprise was ruined, and I still had to come up with a present.

I ended up buying her a pair of sunglasses. I was going to buy her a car, and instead I got her sunglasses. I spent less than fifty dollars instead of tens of thousands of dollars. I watched her open her present and saw tears forming in her eyes. She loved them. She couldn't believe that I got her sunglasses.

I still don't know what to do with all of that. We've worked through it; we're fine now. But what gets me about the whole thing is the response. I had put all this work into finding a car for my wife, and her response was minimal. I put a little work into getting her sunglasses and the response was huge.

●

In Philippians 1:27, Paul says: "Only let your manner of life be worthy of the gospel of Christ."

It's so simple, right? Here is the gospel. Here is some good news—I mean really, really good news! You are forgiven. The holy God who sits above our universe loves *you*. Jesus lived on earth as a human being, He gave His life, He paid for your sins so that you can have a relationship with this holy God. You are going to be with Him forever. And this future is secure because of who Jesus is and what He has done. This is good news!

So how do you respond to that? You should be blown away, right? You should be giddy! You should be on the verge of disbelief because this news is *too* good!

A few nights ago I was trying to remind myself of the gospel. I was preaching the gospel to myself. I told myself, "Francis, you are messed up. You have hurt people. You did wrong in this situation and that situation. You were lost. Beyond hope. And then Jesus *saved* you. He died to pay for everything you've done. He loves you so much that He came down and rescued you. You get to spend eternity with Him!" As I reminded myself of this I was getting so excited, and I couldn't help but think, "Man! The only thing I can do is live a life worthy of this good news!"

Do you remember the first time you fell in love? You get so excited when you find out that this amazing person that you're absolutely in love with actually loves you in return! It's an unbelievable feeling.

Isn't that the way we should respond to the gospel? The gospel calls for a certain response. Paul urges us to live a life that is worthy of the gospel.

Picture an old-fashioned scale in your mind. The two sides of the scale hang in perfect balance when there is no weight on either side. So they would put weights on one side—say five pounds—and then they would put barley on the other side until it evened out. Then they knew they had five pounds of barley.

This is the same idea as having an appropriate response. On one side of the scale you have the incredible news of the gospel. And Paul says, "Your life is on the other side of the scale. Even it out. Make your life worthy of this." The response should be suitable. Your manner of life needs to adequately reflect what you have received.

It comes down to living in light of what we believe. If we really believe that this gospel is so amazing, then our lives should reflect that. But for many of us, we look at the weight of the gospel on the one side, and then we look at the weight of our lives on the other side, and there's no comparison. People would have to look at the scale and say, "No. Those two things don't belong together. They're not equal at all."

•

Earlier in this passage, Paul had said that for him, to live is Christ and to die is gain (1:21). Those are some crazy words. How many of us could repeat that sentence with a straight face? Paul is talking about suffering for Jesus. He wants Jesus so badly that he doesn't care if his enemies kill him because that will just send him into the presence of Christ. He sees suffering as an opportunity to become more like Jesus.

And then Paul turns from describing himself to addressing the Philippians directly. This is the context for Philippians 1:27. And Paul starts this address with the word "only:"

> Only let your manner of life be worthy of the gospel of Christ, so that whether I come and see you or am absent, I may hear of you that you are standing firm in one spirit, with one mind striving side by side for the faith of the gospel, and not frightened in anything by your opponents. This is a clear sign to them of their destruction, but of your salvation, and that from God. (vv. 27–28)

He's basically saying, "I'm only going to ask one thing of you: live a life that's worthy of the gospel. Here's what my life is all about, but all I ask is that your life looks like this."

I read this, and then I look at my life. And I have to be honest with myself. Very often I'm not a good picture of this. The scale isn't balanced. I'm not talking about earning our salvation here; I'm talking about responding appropriately. And I look at the gospel, and the weight of the thing is holding that side of the scale way down. And then I look at myself on the other side of the scale, and the weightlessness of my manner of life is keeping my side of the scale way up in the air. There's nothing equal about it.

I have to ask myself: If I really believed in the weightiness of my salvation, wouldn't I be worshipping so intensely? Wouldn't I be screaming my lungs out? Wouldn't I have trouble sleeping at night because I'm just too excited about this holy God who loves me and sent His Son to die for me?

And then I have to start thinking about other truths in Scripture. In Luke 16 there's a story about a rich man and a poor man named Lazarus. In this story, the rich man ends up in torment—in flames! He begs for mercy and asks that this beggar Lazarus will be sent with a drop of water on the tip of his finger to place on his tongue so he can have a moment's relief from his intense anguish. And here's the crazy thing: I believe that this passage is true. I believe it's real.

So if you put Luke 16 on one side of the scale and my actions on the other side of the scale, are they going to even out? There's no way! And this means that there is inconsistency in my life. There is a disconnect between what I say I believe and how I live my life. If I literally believe that some of the people around me may end up experiencing that sort of anguish, how can I not be doing everything in my power to redirect them?

When you look at my life in light of what I say I believe, my life doesn't make any sense. If you put the Bible on one side of the scale and my life on the other, the scale will not be balanced.

But it should be! I so badly want my life to reflect the truth of the Bible. These days it's so popular to throw certain passages out of the Bible. We find this or that statement offensive, so we toss it. We find a way to explain it away, to say it doesn't belong, to say that it doesn't mean what it says. And so we go through and tear out everything we don't like, and pretty soon the Bible is getting much lighter. Keep throwing Scripture out and pretty soon it will lighten up to the point that the scale will even out. Its weight will match your manner of life.

That will balance the scale, but it's the wrong approach. Why should we be able to take things out of the Bible? It's the Word of God! God doesn't say things He doesn't mean. Don't get me wrong—there are things in the Bible that I would rather not believe. If God had asked my opinion, I might have left some of this out. Some of it is hard to believe. But the thing is, God didn't ask my opinion. It's His Word. He is the source of truth. It really doesn't matter whether it makes sense to me or not. I have no right to pick and choose which parts of the Bible are worth believing. I don't get to select which passages my manner of life should appropriately reflect.

My question for you is, can people look at your life and see that you've been saved and that you are secure in your relationship with God? Can people see joy in your life that stems from knowing the God of the universe?

Think about Matthew 25. It says that Jesus is going to return with all of His angels and all of His glory and He's going to sit on His throne and He's going to be separating people—the sheep from the goats. He's going to look at people and say, "Depart from me, because you didn't feed me when I was hungry or welcome me when I was a stranger." And these people are going to say, "Lord, when did we see you hungry or thirsty or a stranger or naked or sick or in prison?" And Jesus will say, "Because you didn't do it for the least of these, you didn't do it for Me." And with that, those people will be cast into the eternal fire.

Do you believe that? Does your life show that you believe it? Are you living a life worthy of that truth? Could people look at your life and say, "Man, he really believes Matthew 25"?

I've had to look at my life and realize that there are areas in which my life doesn't make any sense.

•

I've heard stories—you've probably heard stories as well—about Christians overseas. I've heard stories about the underground church in China, for example. Or stories about people in India who give their lives to Jesus and literally sacrifice everything. Or I've heard stories about these guys in India that no one really knows about, but somehow they have led millions—I mean, literally millions of people—to the Lord.

I hear some of these stories, and their lives seem to make sense in light of the gospel. I know that my life doesn't make sense, but it seems like the lives of these people do. I have been hearing these stories my whole life, and I finally reached a point where I decided that I had to see for myself. I had to meet some of these Christians around the world. I had to know if they were for real.

So I spent a few months overseas with my family. I didn't do this because I was godly; I did it because I knew I wasn't, but I desperately wanted to be. I looked at my life and saw that I was lacking boldness. I didn't have the guts to say everything God wanted me to say. I was afraid of being rejected. So I wanted to learn from Christians who were bold enough to follow Jesus no matter what it cost.

We travelled first to India, and I had an opportunity to speak to a huge group of people there. You have to understand—these people were the persecuted church. Many of them had watched family members beaten to death for their faith. And there I was, standing on stage in front of all of these people. I didn't know what to say to them. I told them that what I really wanted to do was hear their stories. And that's what I ended up doing.

I listened to a woman tell me about how she came to know the Lord. As soon as her village learned that she was a Christian, the whole village came to her little hut. They brought decapitated lizards and told her that she and her husband needed to drink the blood and convert back to Hinduism. They gave her an ultimatum. She had to deny Jesus.

At this point in the story, this woman looked at me and said, "I couldn't do it. I couldn't deny Jesus." So she grabbed her Bible, and she and her husband just ran. The whole village had rejected them—they would be killed—so they ran into the jungle to hide. She was pregnant with her first child at the time. So as they hid in the jungle, her husband helped her deliver their first child. They were desperate for food for themselves and for this newborn baby. But God provided. He got them through it.

This woman told me, "We weren't going to deny our Lord! I just held on to my Bible. I would not let them take my Bible from me. That was the only thing we grabbed, and we ran."

I talk to a woman like that and I think, *That's a life that's worthy of the gospel. She understands that Jesus is all that matters. Her manner of life is worthy.*

I talked to another guy who showed me the scars on his head and his back. He told me that within a few months of becoming a believer, a huge group of people surrounded him and started beating him. He was thinking, *Okay, God, this is it. This is the way it's going to end. That's okay. But I am not going to deny You!* He told me that he was somehow able to crawl away, but he looked back and watched the crowd beat his friend to death. He endured all of this, and he had only been a follower of Jesus for a few months!

I talked to so many people who went through these kinds of things, and I finally asked one of the leaders, "Don't you have people in your churches who just call themselves Christians but don't really live it out?"

He just looked at me and said, "That wouldn't make any sense. If you call yourself a Christian, you automatically lose everything. Why would someone volunteer for that if they weren't serious?"

This guy told me that when he was eleven years old, he gave his life to Jesus. He told me, "I still remember coming home and telling my dad. It was pouring down rain outside. I told my dad that I was a Christian, and he took everything I had and threw it into the mud. Then he looked at me and said, 'Don't you ever call me Dad again.'"

Think about it. This is an eleven-year-old kid! What would you have done? He said, "I went over and picked my Bible up out of the mud along with a few other items, and I just wandered around looking for somewhere to go." He told me about God's provision and grace over the course of his life. He eventually became a pastor, a husband, and a father. Twenty years later he even reconciled with his dad, who became a believer himself.

This is powerful stuff! I hear these stories and I can't help but think that if this man were on the other side of the scale, his manner of life would be worthy of the gospel.

After India, we went to Thailand. We stayed at a place that was basically an orphanage for kids who had been rescued from sex slavery. Every morning we would wake up and serve these kids. We'd hang out with them and just laugh and play.

At night we would worship together in a little hut. We would be in there with forty or fifty kids while someone played the guitar with minimal skill and led the singing with a less-than-average voice. But no one cared. These kids had their hands in the air, and they were singing at the tops of their lungs! I looked at their faces and realized that these kids understood. My whole family would be in tears thinking about how beautiful this whole thing must be to the Lord. These kids were responding to the God who had literally saved them from a life of slavery. Their lives made sense.

And then we went to China. We visited a part of the underground church where they train leaders. There was a group of eighteen- to twenty-five-year-olds who were being trained as missionaries so they could leave China and serve in the Middle East and other places.

I was getting so fired up as I worshipped and prayed with these young leaders, and then I asked them to share with me about some of the persecution they had endured. But they all looked at me with confused expressions. I said, "I've heard you guys have faced a lot of persecution. Can you tell me what that's like?" Their response was, "Well, yeah. Of course we experience persecution. Doesn't everyone? Didn't Jesus say that they would persecute us just as they persecuted Him? It's just a part of life."

They couldn't understand why I wanted to hear stories about persecution. That was everyday life for them, so they didn't see a point in talking about it. I finally asked them to tell me about just the last time they were persecuted, and they decided to humor me.

One girl said that she was with a group of Christians when government officials came. They all hid as best they could and were basically holding their breath as they heard the officials walking around. They just hoped and prayed that they wouldn't be seen. She told me, "I just kept thinking that this was the way things are supposed to be."

One of the guys said that some government officials showed up while they were meeting and they thought, *There are only three of them but there are fourteen of us.* So they all screamed and started running. The officials started firing their guns but these students knew they were bluffing by shooting into the air. They had been taught in their training to keep running, so that's exactly what they did. And as this guy is telling me his story, he said, "The whole thing was so cool."

As these students shared, I was struck by their joy. They were laughing at each other's stories, and they shared a genuine happiness. I guess I was expecting them to be devoted and passionate—which they were—but I wasn't expecting the joy.

Then they asked me why it was so strange for me to hear their stories. I had to explain that things are different where I came from. I told them that when most Americans talk about the church, they're referring to a building. I explained that we have a ton of these buildings and that you can choose which one you want to attend. Then I told them that people might attend one for a while, but when they find another one with better music they'll switch.

That's when these students started laughing hysterically. I swear I wasn't trying to be funny. Sometimes you're saying something serious and everyone thinks you're joking.

I kept going. I told them that if one church offers better child care than another, then a lot of parents are likely to switch. The students started laughing harder. I explained that sometimes people will switch if the service times are more convenient or if they like one speaker better than another. The students were dying with laughter. I felt like I was doing a comedy routine, but all I was trying to do was explain the American church to the underground church in China.

As they were laughing I realized, *They're right. It doesn't make a lot of sense.* I look at their lives and everything makes perfect sense. I look at our lives and I wonder.

And then you think about the statistics. There are over a billion people in India. China has over a billion people as well. Just those two countries make up about 40 percent of the earth's population. The United States, on the other hand, makes up about 4.6 percent of the earth's population.

When we hear stories of Christians overseas, we think they're weird. But we're the strange ones. This is how Christianity works around the world, and we're over here in America getting caught up in our consumer-driven approach to church.

•

We are the strange ones. Our actions reveal that we think of the church as a building and ourselves as consumers. The rest of the world looks at us and laughs. Where is the disciple making? Where is the commitment? Where is the manner of life that lines up with the gospel?

But many of us are becoming aware of the problem, aren't we? I'm guessing that you look at things in your life and think, *This isn't making sense*. You look at the truth of God's Word and recognize that your life isn't equal to the things you claim to believe. I am praying for a generation that stands firm, understanding that this whole thing is about us following Jesus, suffering for His sake, and making disciples. I am begging God for more and more people that will stop hoping for a pastor that will lead their friends to Christ and instead take the challenge of disciple making head on.

I'm not content with hearing stories of what happens overseas. I want the world to see a group of people who are committed to the gospel of Jesus. I want Christians overseas to get excited about the stories they hear coming out of our churches. I want them to hear about the way we give away our money and possessions even in the midst of a terrible economy because we know that other people are in need. I want them to be inspired by Christians whose lives make sense in light of the Bible.

I'm really not asking anyone to be radical or extreme. I just want your life to make sense. That's what I want for myself as well.

My life made more sense when I was a junior in high school. I remember looking through the yearbook at all of the seniors I knew and feeling overwhelmed at the thought that I might never see these people again. I loved these people and desperately wanted them to know Jesus. So I spent night after night on the phone, just calling these seniors and telling them, "This is probably the weirdest phone call you've ever received, but I may never see you again and I have to say some things to you before it's too late." That kind of thing makes sense for a person who believes in hell.

Or I remember working as a waiter. I had so much fun with my coworkers, but I'd come home and beg God for their salvation. That made sense. I remember my grandmother dying while I tried to scream the gospel into her ear in Chinese. I was such a mess. When she passed I looked over at my brother who wasn't walking with the Lord and told him, "I don't ever want to see you on a hospital bed and not know where you're going. You have to give your life to Jesus! I care about you so much, I don't ever want to be unsure of your salvation." My brother changed his life completely and is now a pastor who trains other pastors.

Those moments made sense in light of what I believe. I want to keep living that type of life. I want to have the peace of being able to look at my life and see that it makes sense.

•

Erwin Lutzer tells a story about man who lived in Germany during the Holocaust. Here is this man's testimony:

> I lived in Germany during the Nazi Holocaust. I considered myself a Christian. We heard stories of what was happening to Jews, but we were trying to distance ourselves from it because what could we do to stop it? A railroad track ran behind our small church, and each Sunday morning we could hear the whistle in the distance and the wheels coming over the tracks. We became disturbed when we heard the cries coming from the train as it passed by. We realized it was carrying Jews like cattle in the cars.
>
> Week after week, the whistle would blow. We dreaded to hear the sound of those wheels because we knew that we would hear the cries of the Jews en route to a death camp. Their screams tormented us. We knew the time the train was coming. And when we heard the whistle blow, we began singing hymns. By the time the train came passed our church, we were singing at the top of our voices. If we heard the screams, we were singing more loudly. And soon we could hear them no more.
>
> Although years have passed, I still hear the train whistle in my sleep. God forgive me. Forgive all of us who call themselves Christians and yet did nothing to intervene.

It's easy to be judgmental when you hear a story like that. How could you hear the cries from a train full of screaming people and try to drown them out by singing your hymns louder?

But when I read that story, I have to ask myself, "Francis, what would you have done? Look at the pattern of your life. Would you really have said something? Would you really have done something? If everyone else was singing, wouldn't you have just sung along?"

I can't say what I would have done. But here's what I would like to see. I would like to see all of us be the kind of people who are willing to stand up and say, "I can't do this anymore! I can't go along with this and pretend that nothing is happening!"

It's easy to look at other moments in history and criticize the church for their poor response. The difficult part is looking at the world right now. I'm not talking about judging the people around you. I'm talking about assessing your own life and being honest before the Lord. Is your manner of life worthy of the gospel?

Paul says:

> Only let your manner of life be worthy of the gospel of Christ, so that whether I come and see you or am absent, I may hear of you that you are standing firm in one spirit, with one mind striving side by side for the faith of the gospel, and not frightened in anything by your opponents. (Philippians 1:27–28)

Isn't that an amazing feeling? To know that your life is worthy of the gospel, to be able to stand firm with the Christians around you, striving side by side for the faith, and not being afraid of anyone? As long as we're focused on ourselves we're going to live as cowards and our lives won't make any sense.

My prayer is that our lives would make sense. My prayer is that we would all have the boldness to honestly assess our lives and ask whether or not we are doing the one thing that Paul urges us to do here. It takes tremendous courage to take this kind of stand. But our brothers and sisters around the world are doing it. It's time we stood alongside them.

15

# We Will Carry the Name

LOUIE GIGLIO

If you've ever climbed mountain peaks, you know there's a huge difference between a high-altitude assent and a casual (or even strenuous) hike. If you use the word *hike* to describe what you're about to do, your major preparation is to decide whether you need a jacket or sunscreen, a water bottle or a trail bar. Hikes are fun. Sure, you might work up a sweat as you stop from time to time to enjoy the views, but there's no serious preparation required. And when you hike you can go straight to the highest point with no need for *acclimatization*. But that's very different from summiting big mountains.

When you're climbing one of the world's great peaks, you don't just bolt to the top. In fact, you can't. It takes months and months of preparation, and then when you get there, it takes weeks, not days, to reach the summit. In fact, if you suddenly found yourself propelled to the top of the world—to a place like the top of Everest—it would take your breath away. Literally. HAPE—high-altitude pulmonary edema—is a condition that occurs when your lungs fill with fluid due to the lack of oxygen. When HAPE sets in, you could die in minutes. Obviously, it's not something that you take casually, or else you most likely could be on your last climb.

Interestingly, there are moments in our Christian experience that feel like that—times when we know we are standing in a sacred space where the routine approach to God takes a turn and suddenly we are on our faces on the ground. I've certainly felt that way at Passion events over the years. That moment when your breath is almost taken away and you know it didn't happen because you were at an event—it happened because you were in the presence of a holy God.

Such encounters happen when you behold the heights of the greatness of the Son of God. You get a glimpse—a tiny burst—of His radiance, and all you want to do is hit the floor. You see this all through Scripture, and once you've been there and experienced it for yourself, you're never really the same.

It's possible our worship needs more moments like these. And to get there we have to gain a new reverence for God. Though He has chosen to come near—and even miraculously dwells in us by the Spirit—*God is not on our level.* We can't just waltz into His presence like we are walking into Starbucks . . . at least not if we want to truly know Him and understand what the Psalmist was talking about when he wrote:

> Who may ascend the mountain of the Lord?
> Who may stand in his holy place? (Psalm 24:3)

If you want to see and know God, you have to draw near as if you were scaling Everest. Not with self-effort and ritualistic success. But soberly and meaningfully as you walk through the valley of His mercy and climb on the grace we have in Jesus Christ.

And when you do get a glimpse of Jesus, He is always central and glorious, eternal and true. Such glimpses are essential to your journey with Christ. If it's true that a host of ten thousand times ten thousand are forever echoing His name, we must have our eyes opened to see that His glory is the greatest reality of all. Jesus is pictured in heaven as a Lamb who takes away the sin of the world. He alone makes possible the payment that erases our debt. He alone gives life that never ends. This is why the angelic beings in His presence never stop saying, "Holy, holy, holy is the Lord God Almighty, who was, and is, and is to come" (Revelation 4:8).

Though seeing Him as He is cannot happen *in full* while you are trapped in fallen flesh, you can see enough to be stunned and amazed. And when it happens, you know that your faith is rooted in more than a hyped-up religious experience, more than talk, more than an event. You know that faith is grounded in something that is real. You know that Jesus is real.

In this life we see through a glass dimly as we faithfully seek to follow Jesus on planet earth. We may dwell in the lowlands, but we have been high enough, often enough to carry something special in our lives as we walk the streets of earth. Having seen Jesus, we come to understand that He is everything. And because He is everything, He is worth everything and demands everything from those who are named after Him. That's what happens when you come into the presence of God, when you rise above the tree line of "ordinary Christianity" and behold the wonder of His face. In these moments you are marked by majesty—captured by grace. And from these moments you know why you are on earth. You know that you were made to know Jesus. And you come to see that you were made to reflect Him to the world.

Is that true of you and me? Have we seen enough of Jesus to be changed by what we have seen?

If the answer is yes, here's what I'd like for us to remember: having tasted and seen His glory, it doesn't matter so much *where* you go; it matters *what* you carry. That's contrary to how most of us spend our energy and thoughts. We spend so much energy and time wondering how to get to the right place in life, don't we? Are we in the right job? Is this the right relationship? Is this the right time frame? You may be asking, am I in the right city? Is this the right educational path? Is this the right house? The sum of all of those questions is really this: What does God want me to do? What is God's will for my life?

If we're not careful, we'll find ourselves paralyzed as we ask that question over and over again. Don't misunderstand me—it's an important question to ask. God cares deeply about the answer to that question and all the others that lead up to it, but He cares about them under a bigger banner, a bigger cause. What matters most to God is not what you do, but *why you do it.* Not where you go, but *what you carry.* In other words, God wants you to carry the right thing with you wherever you go, and when you are carrying the right thing, those other questions become less and less important. And what are we given the opportunity to carry? The name and the fame of Jesus.

It becomes less important whether you spend your life in Bolivia or Birmingham, in Colombia or at Cornell, in East Asia or as a math teacher at East Hills High School, because you can arrive at what you think is the right place yet still carry the wrong thing when you get there. In other words, you can get to the desired place yet become enamored with some other name—the name of a company, a cause, somebody, some pleasure, or even with your own name, position, and accomplishment.

So the question you have to ask yourself is, *What's deep down underneath my happiness?* Is it your job? Your significant other? Your lifestyle? Your location? At some point you are going to reach the point where you are forced to answer the question, *What is driving you to do what you do*? It's amazing that as I have traveled to some of the most remote places on earth and been with people sacrificing everything to do good and serve the "last and least of these," I have found them there with all sorts of strange motives. Though it's easy to see how this would be an inner struggle in a high-profile corporate or culture position, even in some of the most difficult places on earth you can still be motivated by the wrong things. Few things are more miserable than paying a great price to serve God, than doing it to gain approval from Him or someone else, or to make up for mistakes of the past.

But if Jesus is at the source of your happiness, the place and time (and what you do) doesn't matter as much. What matters is that you fall in love with Jesus and with His love for you. And when you do, you will find that He becomes your source of happiness, not what you do or where you go.

So I wonder if we might just put a tiny freeze on the question of what God wants us to do, and instead start asking what He wants us to carry. I think we can learn the answer to that question from the story of Paul.

The story of how Saul became Paul is powerfully recorded for us beginning in Acts 9:

> Meanwhile, Saul was still breathing out murderous threats against the Lord's disciples. He went to the high priest and

> asked him for letters to the synagogues in Damascus, so that if he found any there who belonged to the Way, whether men or women, he might take them as prisoners to Jerusalem. As he neared Damascus on his journey, suddenly a light from heaven flashed around him. He fell to the ground and heard a voice say to him, "Saul, Saul, why do you persecute me?"
>
> "Who are you, Lord?" Saul asked.
>
> "I am Jesus, whom you are persecuting," he replied. "Now get up and go into the city, and you will be told what you must do." (Acts 9:1–6)

It's just an ordinary day for Saul, doing what he was in the practice of doing. He was hell bent on getting rid of this start-up religion, at that time called "The Way"—those who claimed that Jesus had died and risen again. He was traveling to Damascus to round up any men or women who believed these things so that he could throw them in jail back in Jerusalem. But suddenly and unexpectedly everything changed. Jesus appeared to him and asked Saul a question: "Why are you persecuting me?" Saul responded with another question: "Who are you, Lord?" It makes me wonder how Saul, if he didn't know who he was talking to, could call him "Lord." But given that he was standing face to face with the risen Son of God, I think I understand. Saul had just been dropped out of a helicopter on top of Everest. Maybe the fluid was filling his lungs. His breath was short, and he didn't know what else to say.

Jesus' answer is beautiful in its simplicity, isn't it? "I am Jesus," He answered, "the one you are persecuting." Jesus wanted Saul to understand not only who He was, but also that Saul wasn't just going after some random people in Damascus. Saul was actually persecuting Jesus Himself.

If we can make a brief stop here, there is a huge lesson to be learned about carrying the name of Jesus. Simply put—we will, at times, be persecuted for the name of Jesus. His name is not like any other. The name of Jesus holds the power to save and makes demons tremble. That's important for you to remember if you want to carry the right thing. You must remember that they are not persecuting you, but the Christ whose name you carry.

If we find ourselves in a situation where we are being persecuted, let's make sure that it's Jesus who is being persecuted and not the fact that we are annoying in the way we present Him to the world. More times than not, that's exactly what's happening. We're the ones who put the gospel tracts down instead of the tips at restaurants. We're the ones who are constantly critical of others. We're the ones who are always talking and never listening. We are the ones who don't know when to inject the Name and when to wait patiently for the right opportunity. We are insolent and not understanding, sometimes badgering and not always serving. So when we get persecuted, it's not because of Jesus; it's often because of us.

Our goal is, as Paul would later write, to as much as possible live at peace with everyone. As much as possible be all things to everybody. As much as possible, we want to be winsome and attractive to the world. But even in doing that, at some point Christ is going to be our source and the topic of our conversation, and some people aren't going to like that. If that's the case, then we just have to live with it and know that God is above the critics and He can defend Himself. But if it's us that is causing the rub, we need to ask God to adjust our hearts so we can more effectively carry this precious gift of Jesus' name to our world.

So what did Jesus say to Saul? Pretty simple—get up and go to the city. It was evidently a pretty short meeting. The problem was that Saul had been to the heights, and because he had, his body short-circuited. He got up unable to see, blinded by a glimpse of the Son of God. For three days, Saul couldn't see and didn't eat or drink anything.

So let's resume the story:

> In Damascus there was a disciple named Ananias. The Lord called to him in a vision, "Ananias!"
>
> "Yes, Lord," he answered.
>
> The Lord told him, "Go to the house of Judas on Straight Street and ask for a man from Tarsus named Saul, for he is praying. In a vision he has seen a man named Ananias come and place his hands on him to restore his sight." (Acts 9:10–12).

That's pretty specific, isn't it? So God does give Ananias a specific mission, and He will do that for you. But the goal wasn't just that Ananias get to the right address, but that he carry the right message when he arrived.

Ananias, for his part, is a little concerned. He knows about this guy. He's heard the rumors. So he wants a little confirmation from God: "Are you sure? I just want to be positive that you said Saul of *Tarsus* and not Saul of *Carsus*. Because I'm sure it's on your radar, but this guy has come here with governmental authority to round up all the people who call on the name of Jesus."

Yep—God is sure, and listen to what He says:

> "Go, for he is a chosen instrument of mine to carry my name before the Gentiles and kings and the children of Israel. For I will show him how much he must suffer for the sake of my name." (Acts 9:15–16 ESV)

Did you catch it? This man Saul, who was an enemy of Jesus yet had been transported to the heights in His presence, this hater of the faith and destroyer of the cause, would be God's chosen instrument to "carry My name." Saul—who was vehemently opposed to the name of Jesus—was now being chosen to *carry that very Name.* In time he would write the bulk of the New Testament under God's inspiration, become the church planter of church planters, and stand before kings. And what God was planning for him is what God is planning for you—that whether you go to Ghana or Goldman Sachs, whether you work in Namibia or NYC, you would be a carrier of the name of Jesus Christ wherever you go.

It's interesting that Saul/Paul wasn't chosen to just carry the gospel, carry the message, carry Christianity, carry the faith. He, like us, was chosen to carry The Name.

Understand the gravity of that statement. The Jews in the olden times wouldn't even write the name of God in the Scripture. In the latter days, when the Essenes were holed up in the caves of Qumran copying the Old Testament, they would treat the name of God with such care that when they came to it in Scripture, they would get up from the table, go to the ritual bath, wash themselves, come back to the table, pick up a brand-new quill, write the name of God, put the pen down never to be used again, go from the table again, wash themselves until they were ceremonially clean, and come back again to start writing. That's the kind of care they would use in treating the name of God.

Yet in these last days, God has made His name visible and tangible and knowable to you and me, and that name is Jesus—the most precious name of all. And God says that's what you're going to carry to the world. Wherever you go, whatever you're doing, and whoever you're doing it with, God's intent for you is to be a name carrier of Jesus Christ. Though that name stands alone in majesty and power, and carrying it is something that should cause you to stand in awe, in reality you are amazingly well suited for the job. You are a fantastic name carrier, and you do it all the time. Because with each new generation there are new names to be championed to the world.

Think about the names we currently carry every single day:

Mumford and Sons. The Killers. Fun. Katy Perry. Rihanna. Kings of Leon. Pink. Taylor Swift. Daft Punk. Vampire Weekend. Zach Brown. Lady Gaga. Beyonce. Jay'Z. One Direction. JT. Luke Bryan. Bruno Mars. Blake. Justin. I mean seriously, it's quite possible that many of us have carried one of these names in recent days, and there are hundreds of others we could add to the list.

Have you carried any of these today?

Then there's also ESPN. Bravo. Food TV. Spotify. iTunes. YouTube.

And the brands: Urban. Anthropologie. North Face. Polo. Cole Haan. Lacoste. Coach. Gucci. Abercrombie. Louis Vuitton. Dooney & Bourke. Fossil. Vera Bradley. Kenneth Cole. Donna Karan. Kate Spade. Lucky. Oakley. MAC. Timberland. American Eagle. Lululemon. Ray-Ban. Guess. Diesel. Nike. Chuck Taylor. Toms. Levi Strauss. Adidas. New Era. Joe's. Michael Kors. Calvin Klein. And on and on and on. It's likely that a lot of you are actually carrying/wearing one of these names right now.

We could fill this chapter, and even this book, with all the names. PS3. Xbox. Apple. Kobe. Lebron. Brady. Baptist. Methodist. The Pope. Fallon. Conan. Oprah. Add to them our favorite Christian bands and worship leaders, the preachers, authors, and podcasters. It's overwhelming how many names cross our lips every day! So. Many. Names.

Here's the thing—all those people, stores, and products have one thing in common:

*They are counting on you to carry their name.*

They may not know why, but they know you are a great name-carrier, and they are depending on you. If you don't carry their names, they go broke. The good news for them is that many of you are up for it, day in and day out, because it's complicated trying to untangle yourselves from the web of marketing you live in. You wear the clothes, play the games, rep the stores, and cheer for the teams. You carry the names of the day. But your life was meant for something more.

You can determine what you carry. And what God is saying to Ananias about Paul is that he is going to carry the name that's above all the others.

If you keep reading Acts 9, you see that Ananias does what God asked him to do. He goes to the house on Straight Street, finds Paul, lays his hands on him, prays, and the scales fall from his eyes and he can see again. Immediately, Paul has something to eat, heads to the synagogue, and starts to preach the name of Jesus. And he never, ever stops.

He lives up to the name. He proclaims the name. He preaches the name. And, eventually, he dies for the name of Jesus.

This awesome, powerful, majestic, holy God is looking to you to carry the name of Jesus. Let's be clear here, because there's a difference between carrying the name of Jesus and what often passes for carrying the name of Jesus. This doesn't mean promoting an event. It doesn't mean broadcasting your particular ministry involvement. It doesn't mean quoting your favorite teacher or author, though there are some great ones out there. We, at Passion, are fortunate enough to be associated with some great names.

Some big names on the Christian landscape. But if all we ever talk about is Passion, or somebody, then we've missed it. Some in the Christian world may clamor around those names, but let's face it, deep down people are searching for more. The world—while infatuated by earthly names—is dying to hear about the name that has the power to save and the name that dispels darkness. The name that can restore what's been lost and repair what's been broken. The name that can truly fill the human heart without leaving it shattered and empty the following day. That's the name of Jesus, and, amazingly, you hardly ever hear many church people actually talking about Him.

There is a chance—even a very good chance—that most of us will one day turn around and realize that an entire lifetime has slipped through our fingers and all we ever did was carry the names of the products, icons, institutions, and culture makers of our generation. Sadly, we will see we were mere mules for the culture though we were given the astonishing privilege of carrying *The Name* that outlasts them all.

But there is another option. For years at Passion, we have gathered around the banner of Isaiah 26:8: "Yes, Lord, walking in the way of your truth we eagerly wait for you, for Your name and renown are the desire of our souls." Your name. Your renown.

When all those other names have passed away, there will only be one name still standing. One name that outshines them all. One name that will drive every knee to the ground and cause every tongue to confess His greatness. One name that has the power to bring the dead to life. Don't you want to be a part of the people that are passionate about carrying that name?

But you probably won't carry the name very far or very well just because you know it's the right thing to do, will you? We carry the name because we have had an encounter with Jesus. A heart-wrecking, idol-crushing, soul-exploding encounter with the real and living Jesus. You're going to carry a name with you. Make sure it's the right one.

You don't have to strive or strain. You simply reflect the light of His glory that is shining on you.

> I have seen you in the sanctuary and beheld your power and your glory.
> Because your love is better than life, my lips will glorify you.
> I will praise you as long as I live, and in your name I will lift up my hands.
> I will be fully satisfied as with the richest of foods; with singing lips my mouth will praise you. (Psalm 63:2–5)

To put it simply, God's will for your life is to carry His name wherever you go, in whatever you do, in whichever circumstances you find yourself. Go sculpt. Go be a philanthropist. Go work with kids in the slums of Africa. Go build wells in India. Go to Hollywood or Dollywood. Go be a middle school PE teacher. Go be a doctor. Go work for Google, or Goodwill, or Grace Church. Go to Goldman Sachs for crying out loud. *Go, go, go!* Follow your passion. Pursue the path of your giftedness. Do what keeps you up at night and makes your heart come alive! It doesn't matter where; it matters what you're carrying as you go.

And when you carry His glory on your face as you go, you will automatically make whatever you do about Jesus. Because His goodness is the rock bottom of your life and joy no matter what, you will always be in the right place making a huge difference.

You'll be using life for what matters most, not losing your life because you are making it all about some other name that is fleeting and frail.

Nothing you will ever possess will eclipse the value of what you now have been entrusted to carry as a follower of Jesus. You have arrived at the world's highest peak, a personal relationship with the Maker of it all.

16

# Let's Work It Out

LOUIE GIGLIO

Music has always been a vital part of Passion, but it's not just singing songs for the sake of singing songs. For us, the music is a way to raise our banner—to lift up anthems for a generation that is marching to the same beating heart of God. Our songs not only touch people in unique and powerful ways that mere words do not, they underscore and amplify our message. Our music moves us, but it also teaches us, and it has always been that way.

But you also see the same thing in the history of the Church. So much of God's truth is recorded in the medium of psalms and hymns. These were intended to be sung or read aloud, not so that God's people would have a catchy tune, but so they could connect deeply with the truths of God, remember them, and pass them along to the next generation. And the psalms are not the only places in Scripture this is true. In fact, Philippians 2 was probably one of the earliest songs sung by the Church following the resurrection. It's a psalm that rivets our focus on Jesus.

The church at Philippi had its struggles, just like any church made up of people. One of the things these believers were struggling with was clarity—or focus. And it's pretty much the same today. What are you thinking about and focusing on? Who or what captivates your attention? Where does your gaze fall? Is it mostly on you or on Jesus?

This is an important question for you because if your focus is on you, it will eventually create division among those around you. Selfishness is at the heart of almost every bit of strife in our lives. Yet, Jesus is selfless in the way He gives His life away for you. So if your gaze is on Him, you will treat others as He is treating you. Here's how Paul put it:

> Therefore if you have any encouragement from being united with Christ, if any comfort from his love, if any common sharing in the Spirit, if any tenderness and compassion, then make my joy complete by being like-minded, having the same love, being one in spirit and of one mind. Do nothing out of selfish ambition or vain conceit. Rather, in humility value others above yourselves, not looking to your own interests but each of you to the interests of the others. (Philippians 2:1–4)

To be others focused is a revolutionary, world-shaking concept, especially since we live in a day and time when our gaze falls almost exclusively on the mirror. Most all our decisions, time, and resources are geared ultimately toward ourselves. With this kind of thinking, other people simply become a means to us getting what we want or us feeling better about ourselves. However, if you remember how you are united with Christ, and what His life and love mean to you, you can look beyond yourself to see and meet the need in someone else.

What would life be like if you started considering others more important than yourself? If you truly placed others' needs before your own? Not out of a desire to be seen as "others focused," but because you truly were rooted in the love of Christ and had something to give. Not only would it jar you from the central position in the story, a place our flesh longs for—but one that is best occupied by Jesus—it would put you in a posture where God can really use you. Can you imagine how different and beautiful our family—the Church—would be if we were all living this way?

But Paul knows this is a pretty high bar he has set. So he gives you an example to follow, and the example is the Son of God.

In your relationships with one another, have the same mind-set as Christ Jesus:

> Who, being in very nature God, did not consider equality with God something to be used to his own advantage; rather, he made himself nothing by taking the very nature of a servant, being made in human likeness. And being found in appearance as a man, he humbled himself by becoming obedient to death—even death on a cross! (Philippians 2:6–8)

Now that's a great song. As the early church would sing these words together, they were reminded of the uniqueness, humility, and supremacy of Jesus. The words are rich, Christ-centric and are dripping with solid theology.

Listen to what the song teaches us. Jesus was in very nature God, yet He didn't hoard or cling to His Deity. Rather, He emptied Himself and took on flesh, He humbled Himself and took up the cross. Jesus didn't need anyone, rather He chose to humble Himself. And further, Jesus surrendered in obedience to the plans and purposes of God. Jesus wasn't just *a little* obedient, He was obedient to the point of death. Jesus gave it all. And not just any kind of death. His was one of the worst deaths imaginable—death on a cross. Jesus gave up His life and died on the symbol of guilt and shame, bearing the full wrath of the righteous justice of God because of our sin.

Paul is saying, set your attention on Him. Shape your mindset around Jesus. Think and act like He did.

*Woah!* Astonishing.

The song continues:

> Therefore God exalted him to the highest place and gave him the name that is above every name, that at the name of Jesus every knee should bow, in heaven and on earth and under the earth, and every tongue acknowledge that Jesus Christ is Lord, to the glory of God the Father. (Philippians 2:9–11)

In the church tradition I grew up in, there would most certainly be a hearty "amen" inserted here. And there should be. Jesus is exalted. He holds the highest title in the universe. All of heaven says amen. But the song doesn't stop there. And what comes next seals the deal. Instead of a period after the phrase "and every tongue acknowledge that Jesus Christ is Lord," there is a comma of great significance. The verse continues, "that every knee will bow and every tongue will confess that Jesus Christ is Lord **COMMA** to the glory of God the Father." That comma changed my life, and in the meaning of that comma Passion was born. That comma represents what we are rooted in and living for—that all things exist and all things have been done for God's glory. Are you with me?

To truly live you must awaken to the reality of the comma.

You must come alive to the overarching purpose of the entire universe—which is the glory of God. Yes, Christ came. And surely Christ humbled Himself. Christ died, was raised, and was lifted up again with the name above all others and with ultimate authority. All people will bow to His name. Every tongue will acknowledge Him. Everyone who has ever lived will recognize that Jesus Christ is Lord, and that is all going to happen to the end that the greatness of God is put on display. This will bring glory to the God of gods, who's unlike any other god who has ever been seen or heard. It will bring praise to the One who comes for us, and surrenders for us, who dies in our place and raises us up to live again. The work of Christ did something *for* us, but all the glory is *to* God. And here, my friends, is where the "amen" belongs!

Do you see it? Your life finds ultimate meaning inside that comma—in the reality that you are living in a story much bigger than you. This truth single-handedly explodes your brief you-story and jettisons you into the epic story of God. Soon you see every day, every opportunity, every decision as a chance to shine a light on Him. You start trying to figure out what will bring the most glory to Him in every situation. But how do you get there?

Interestingly, the next verse opens with the word *therefore.* When you see this word, you always have to ask what it is *there for.* In this case, the *therefore* refers to you coming alive to the reality of who Jesus is and what He means to your life. You see that He has literally laid down His life to give you yours. When the power of that truth leaves the category of information and becomes personal to you in revelation (meaning your eyes have opened and the truth has moved from your brain to the core of who you are, your heart), stuff starts to change. For us at Passion, this shift is the core and what we are hoping will happen to you. We are hoping you will experience a theological shift that moves you from *me* to *He*. A change in which you die to a life that's all about you, and Christ comes to life within you.

When that shift happens in you, your goals change. Your dreams and ambitions are altered. You no longer operate in a religious system of who's better or worse, where your goal is to be just a little bit holier than the next person. Your goal is no longer to be just a tad more moral than your roommate, to be just a little more committed than some other family in your church, or more globally minded than your friends. The goal for you is to live a life that mirrors Jesus—to have the same way of thinking in your mind as Christ has in His. That's the new standard and the new goal for your life.

Your aim is to think like He thinks, to see like He sees, to react and respond the way Christ reacts and responds. Notice, Paul is not saying, "I want to say a few things to you and make some suggestions for your lives." He is holding out the Son of God and saying, "Follow Him. Do, think, and live as He did, and do it all for the glory of God."

You might say that the strength of Passion is really measured in the "therefore"—in what happens next. Because it's not whether we are able to gather thousands of people at a given time that matters; it's whether something real happens in our midst and in our hearts that sends us back to where we came from joyfully determined to live mightily for the glory of God.

At one time Paul had lived among the Philippians and led and loved them. But now he was gone. Reaching back to encourage them, he writes, "Therefore, my dear friends, as you have always obeyed—not only in my presence, but now much more in my absence—continue to work out your salvation with fear and trembling, for it is God who works in you to will and to act in order to fulfill his good purpose" (Philippians 2:12–13). In other words, never forget what happened when you came to know Christ, and keep working out the life that He has placed within you.

You and I, it seems, are always wanting more from God. We constantly ask for more of this and more of that—more blessing here and more blessing there. It's true we should always seek to know God more, but Paul says that what we need is not more input, but more output—more of God's life and power flowing from and through our lives to the world. Of course it's not wrong to keep depending on God for His power and provision over our lives. He says, "Ask and you will receive." But at some point we have to come to terms with the fact that God has already given us more blessing than we know what to do with. We have to realize what He has already deposited in our accounts and who He is in our lives and start acting like something has changed—because it has. Paul reminds us in Ephesians 1 that we have already been given every spiritual blessing in Christ. God has held nothing back from us. Christ has come for us. Christ has died to set us free. And Christ is risen to the heights and invites us to share in His story, power, glory, and plan.

You are not normal anymore—you are His and everything has changed. He has given you His Son. Placed in you the Holy Spirit. Placed in your hands the Word. Graced you with a spiritual family and a place at His table. God has given you a new name and birthed His very nature inside of you. He's given you wisdom and clarity, confidence and hope. What He has given you is more than enough for a lifetime of serving Him and touching the world in His name. So much more has gone in than has come out. *Therefore*, we are to work out what God has already placed within!

There might be part of you that bristles at that notion. I mean, our story is all about grace, right? We don't want to get caught up in anything that sounds like work! True, up to a point. But you see there is a big difference between Paul challenging you to work *for* your salvation and his challenge for you to work *out* your God-given salvation. The only way you work out your salvation is through beginning to embrace the grace that is already working in you.

Trust in the reality that God is already working in you long before you start thinking about working anything out. Paul says you are to work out your salvation, but he immediately tells us how we do that. Again, we work out our salvation the same way God worked it into us in the first place—by His grace.

Living with the rhythm of this grace is far better than trying to rely on yourself. Because in the same way that you were powerless to save yourself, you are still powerless on your own to effect any real change in your life. Have you noticed this to be true in your life? Do you have trouble doing the things you know you want to do and not doing the things you don't want to do? Welcome to life apart from the power of God. With this way of living, our best hope is to double down on our self-effort and keep on the merry-go-round of rededications, hoping one day something will stick for longer than a few days.

That's the usual cycle of the Christian experience. You come to an event like Passion, you feel the conviction of God on your life, so you "rededicate" your life. You walk down an aisle or raise your hand. You say some prayer, you build a bonfire, you "transfer" your sin to a stick and throw it in the fire. Or maybe you write all your wrongs on a slip of paper and nail the paper to a makeshift cross. It's not that there's anything wrong with any of these things. I've been there and done them, too. But essentially what you're doing in these commitment times is hoping and promising that you'll never commit that sin again.

And for a little while you don't.

But then you do.

And at some point you have to rededicate your rededication. Have you ever done that? Have you ever prayed one of those prayers that went something like: *God, I know I told you last time that I would never, ever do this again. But this time I really mean it. This time will be the very last time, and I will never have this conversation with you again. I mean it. I promise.*

But, at some point you do.

That is a huge drag. And at the end of the day all this rededication approach does is take the wind out of your sails and remove the hope that Christianity is viable for you. Secretly you start to wonder if there is something wrong with the faith, with you, or both.

But a freeing change happens when you stop the rededications and admit your inability to really follow through in a lasting way. When that happens, you find a God waiting there who says, "I am the One who is at work in you to will and to do My good pleasure." I absolutely love the juxtaposition of these two verses. In one we are shoved out of the bunker of me and mine and told to do something with the faith God has put in us. But in the next breath we are reassured that the only way we are going to do anything with the life that God has put in us is by the same means that life was put in us to begin with. Our lifeline is the working and willing power of God in us. So we trade our willpower for God's willpower, our effort for His.

So what does this look like for you? Not like the old pattern of rededication, but the new pathway of surrender. And it's not something you do occasionally at a conference or retreat. It's not something you do once in life and move on from it. Surrender becomes your way of life, a moment by moment breathing in and out saying, "Jesus, my will is frail and my power small. Will You do what I cannot do? Right now. Right here, in this moment. I'm surrendering to You."

I remember the time in my life as a college student when I started waking up to the staggering beauty of this truth. I would walk through downtown Atlanta, meditating on a single phrase: Jesus, I can't, but You can. For me, saying it over and over again was a reminder that living the Christian life wasn't about trying harder, making promises I was bound to break over and over again. But following Jesus is about me dying to the self-effort—over and over again—that doesn't work and letting go of my ability to do anything at all to improve my situation. For me, it was about taking up, by faith, the power of God who is working in me to accomplish His good pleasure, and trusting Him moment by moment to supply all the power that I needed. And sometimes, you don't even begin by asking God to help you change. You begin where you are and ask Him to give you the "want to" that you don't have.

When we work out our salvation, we do so by trusting that God actually will indeed do what He says He will do. That's really good news and what drives the things Paul writes next:

> Do everything without grumbling or arguing, so that you may become blameless and pure, "children of God without fault in a warped and crooked generation." Then you will shine among them like stars in the sky. (Philippians 2:14–15)

I love the word *everything.* Paul is urging you to simplify your life to this one idea: God is working His life into you, and He is working His life out of you. Given that, why would you ever complain, grumble, or argue with anyone? On the contrary, you say, "God, if You are willing to live your life through me, then what do I have to complain about? Life may be hard, but You live in me." This is not some reluctant obedience, but it is a shift of heart that will cause us to stand out in a complaining and grumbling world, one that is full of dissatisfied people who are always clamoring for something they don't have. To know what you have, and to live it out, frees you from the clatter and will cause you to shine like an incandescent bulb on a pitch-dark night. You become blameless and pure and glow like a star in the sky.

In light of this passage, one of the things I want you to see very clearly is that there is still something to be said for living a life of purity for the sake of Jesus. We live in a day and time when Christian liberty is being flaunted and exploited to the point that it is ceasing to be liberty and starting to be license. I remember seeing a social media post a while back from a college student that said, "Passion rocked," and the very next post read, "Man, I got hammered Saturday night."

What we need to recover is the call to actually live like Jesus in the midst of a generation that's crooked and going the wrong way. It's wonderful that at Passion we can gather thousands of people in one place under the banner of the name of Jesus, but there are millions and millions of others surrounding us every day where everything is crooked and very little is satisfyingly true and right. What we need more than a gathering is for a few students who are willing to work out what God is working in. What we need are people who are willing to translate all this "conference goodness"—by the power and grace of God who is at work within them—into real life and begin walking it out in the middle of a perverse generation. Not to walk around judging the world, but to walk through it shining brightly.

The real story of Passion isn't going to be told in arenas, it's going to be told thousands of times over in the individual worlds and circles of influence of those who are willing to reflect in real life what's happened inside them at Passion.

Several years ago, there was a TV show that took the United States by storm called *Extreme Makeover: Home Edition.* If you're not familiar with the show, the idea is that a bus full of contractors and a host of volunteers descend upon the home of a family that's down on their luck. So while the family spends the week at Disney World or some other destination, this amazing collection of builders, designers, and volunteers demolish and rebuild their home for free. And at the end of every show, there is the big reveal.

The family comes back from Disney in a limo and pulls up in front of their completely rebuilt home. But there is a tour bus blocking their view. The suspense builds throughout the show as they are asked if they want to see their new home. And then the host of the show shouts these three words: "Move that bus!" This is the big moment—the moment the family finally gets to see all the work that's been done. And though you've been waiting through the show to see the house from street view, that's not what the camera focuses on. It focuses instead on the faces of the family. Mom, dad, their seven adopted kids and three foster children—that's what you see.

But it's not that you don't see the house at that moment; you do! You just see it on the faces of the family as they shriek and laugh, cry, and stand in awe. You are able to see just how great what's been built is by observing those who now see it, and you see the beauty of the house in their expressions. When you eventually do see the house, it's no big surprise as to how awesome it is. You've already seen its glory reflected in the family. This is what it looks like to work out what God has been working in.

Some of your friends and coworkers haven't seen Jesus yet. They don't know about His greatness. They haven't had their eyes opened to His perfect nature, His obedience, His death, or His rise to the highest name in heaven and on earth. But you know what they can see? They can see your face. And they know by looking at you when you start working out the greatness of what God has been working inside you that you're beholding something big. Something massive. Something life changing. That's what you are called to do—to work it out as God works in you to will and do His good pleasure. When you do, there is no doubt about who will get the glory. You will get the life change, and He will get the glory.

# Notes

**Chapter 2**

1. C. S. Lewis, "Meditation in a Toolshed," in *C. S. Lewis: Essay Collection and Other Short Pieces* (London: Harper Collins, 2000), 60.

**Chapter 4**

1. www.ALZ.org.
2. December 19, 2010.

**Chapter 11**

1. C. S. Lewis, "The Weight of Glory," in *The Weight of Glory and Other Addresses* (Grand Rapids: William B. Eerdmans Publishing Company, 1965), 10.

For more resources from
Passion and Louie Giglio please visit
passionresources.com